From My Hands

By Olwyn Horwood

GPL GEORGESON PUBLISHING LIMITED

FROM MY HANDS

Publisher's Note

The designs in this book were made using fabric and threads available in retail shops in New Zealand. As publisher, we are aware that some of these items may not be found in your local shop, so every effort has been made to include alternative materials that can be found in specialist needlework retailers in your country. We believe and know that the alternatives suggested will give very satisfactory results, and most importantly in the end, a beautiful piece of needlework to be cherished for years to come. As always we welcome your letters, email messages and telephone calls. The messages we receive from everywhere needlework is enjoyed brighten our day! Please let us know how you progress through this book.

Prue Georgeson

Published by Georgeson Publishing Limited
P.O. Box 100667, North Shore Mail Centre, New Zealand 1330
Ph: 649 410 2079 Fax: 649 410 2069
Email: gpl@georgeson.co.nz web site www.georgeson.co.nz

This book is copyright. Except for the purpose of fair reviewing, no part of this publication may be reproduced or transmitted in any form or by any means, electronic or mechanical, including photocopying, recording, or any information storage and retrieval system, without permission in writing from the publisher. Infringers of copyright render themselves liable to prosecution

ISBN 0 9582105-0-0

© (1999) Georgeson Publishing Limited

Editor: Prue Georgeson
Photography: Maria Sainsbury
Illustrations: Gabriella Klepacki
Layout: Andreena Buckton of Noodle Design Corp.

Printed in Hong Kong

CONTENTS

Introduction	4
General Notes	5
Stitches	10
Bookmarks	22
Pink Simplicity	27
Sweet Lavender	32
Danish Coaster	36
Louisa's Opal	40
Photographs	49
A Tribute to Miss M.E. Roe	57
Needlework Accessories	64
A Danish Christmas	72
Paua Lights	80
Blue Horizons	88
Danish Handkerchief	95

FROM MY HANDS

Introduction

I have stitched all my life. To me it is not really a choice it is a necessity - for my peace of mind and enjoyment of life.

My fondness for pulled thread embroidery started at secondary school when I stitched a tablecloth in cream on cream and I have not stopped since then! I have been fortunate to be encouraged by the late Margaret Ohms, friends at Auckland and North Shore Guilds, other Guilds throughout New Zealand and also around the world. Thanks also to the many, many needleworkers over the years who have contributed to the dozens of classes I have held. Teaching this work is a pleasure.

I believe that this book of counted satin stitch combined with pulled thread techniques offers a wonderful opportunity for those who might not have tried this type of work before to start now, and also for those who already enjoy this work, to progress to new levels! We are all used to counting threads for cross stitch and the joy in moving into this embroidery is that a different but very achievable technique is learnt. It also has the advantage that no threads are cut or withdrawn in its execution so that it is a technique one can relax and enjoy. To correct the odd mistake is easy.

It is embroidery that is elegant in appearance, uncluttered and very stylized. I really enjoy the feeling I get of carrying on a stitching tradition from the past – a link with needlewomen who went before me and those who will come after me.

I hope you share my point of view when you have worked some of the designs in this publication.

Olwyn Horwood

FROM MY HANDS

General Notes

Pulled Thread Embroidery is a quickly learned technique in which *no threads are withdrawn* in the working of the embroidery, instead the fabric is pulled together with stitchery. This embroidery is also referred to as 'drawn fabric work'.

The origins of pulled thread embroidery can be traced back to the seventeenth century when taxes on the importation of laces from France were introduced in many countries in Europe. The loss of the much admired French laces spurred the embroiderers in the different countries affected by these taxes to develop their own forms of embroidery closely allied to needlepoint lace. These are today described as drawn fabric or pulled thread work, whitework and Dresden work.

Eventually many countries produced their own type of whitework along with their own style of colourful traditional embroidery. For example: Russia, India, Greece, Czechoslovakia, Spain, Turkey Sicily and South America. Top clothing and embroidery for the house was usually decorated with strong colours and household linen and undergarments were usually worked in self coloured embroidery. The different countries produced embroidery that was unique to their area. It was used on handkerchiefs (fichus), aprons, caps, cascading cuffs and petticoat flounces and great quantities of this embroidery were produced.

When doing pulled thread work the hallmark of expert embroidery is evenness of tension with no distortion of the overall shape of the fabric. The work is clean and uncluttered in appearance with the negative (unstitched) space as important as the worked area of the design.

I particularly enjoy studying work from the past. Many times I 'see' ideas for my stitching from a wide array of different sources. Postcards from museums featuring old embroidery, books and magazines from the turn of the century and earlier. Ethnic weaving patterns are also a rich source of ideas, as are bridal and trousseau wear. Museums sometimes have collections of beautiful old embroidery and these are a great source of inspiration also.

Pulled thread embroidery holds an irresistible fascination for embroiderers and its charms today are becoming more and more appreciated as its delicate lacy appearance in no way impairs its strength because the threads of the material are not withdrawn to weaken the fabric.

Use of Charts

Each line equals one thread on every chart in this book.
Satin stitch designs, where a stitch is ended and a new stitch started and both stitches are in a straight line the break in the stitch is indicated by a dotted line through the stitches.

How to Stitch

Most stitches are worked as a sewing stitch, in and out of the material in one movement, not as a stab stitch. The most important factor is an even technique and this comes with practise.

GENERAL NOTES

Tacking

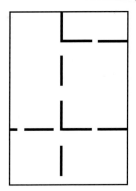

It is extremely important to tack accurately over and under the number of threads specified in each pattern. Stitch the first line of tacking from side to side across the linen in one direction. Make sure when tacking to mark the centre that your threads *meet at the centre,* but do not cross over the tacking stitch, as this gives you an exact point to count from. To ensure this happens, tack from top to bottom, then starting at the centre, tack to the left, leaving a long thread dangling at the centre. Complete the tacking on the left hand side, finish and then go back to the centre, rethread the needle and tack out to the right hand side. All lines must cross at right angles with the stitch coming out in the same space as the previous stitch.

Equipment required

Embroidery Frame
A frame is essential to get even tension on every stitch. The top ring of the frame should just grip the material holding the work secure. If it is pushed on too tightly it will flatten and fluff the work underneath. Have the material with a bit of 'give' in the frame. (see page 52 for a photograph of my work in a frame)

Stiletto
A Stiletto is very useful when working circular eyelets. On the completion of each eyelet a gentle push to extend the centre to an even round shape creates a perfect eyelet

Laying Tool
It is important to keep the threads smooth in satin stitch for a really beautiful finished appearance. A laying tool can be purchased and used to keep the threads in place side by side while pulling the threads through the fabric. Hold the laying tool inside the loop of the working thread, when the loop is about 5 cm (2 in) from the material put tension on the loop by gently moving the laying tool back and forward to allow the threads to move and lie evenly.

Then pull the stitch through the fabric keeping the threads side by side against the laying tool. This should result in a stitch with a nice smooth appearance and no twisted threads!

My laying tool has a little rounded 'knob' on the end which means that the threads do not slip off the end before I want them to! A tapestry needle or large bodkin can be used as alternatives.

Scissors
You really need two pairs of scissors. One a small pair with sharp points and fine blades for cutting threads and a second larger pair for more general cutting, snipping, and trimming edges.

Glasses
Like many others who stitch I do not have perfect eyesight. I am short sighted so I wear glasses at all times. I do not find the need for clip on magnifying lenses or a magnifying lamp, unless working on fabric with more than 40 threads to the inch, however if you have difficulty doing this work I would recommend that you consider these. It is important to be able to see the threads easily and comfortably.

Needles

For the majority of the embroidery done in pulled thread work Size 24 or 26 tapestry needles are ideal. Size 28 tapestry needles are now available and I use these with the fine thread e.g. Zwicky, Guterman etc. The blunt 'point' will not split the threads of the material and will give the work an even and precise look. The finer the fabric the finer the needle to be used. However when starting and finishing it can be most useful to have a sharp needle or a size 8 - 10 Crewel needle which has a big eye but sharp point.

Linen

There are many high quality linen fabrics around for you to use when stitching these beautiful designs and as you will be putting many hours of work into stitching, it is important that you use fabrics and threads worthy of the effort involved in their creation.

I use linens with a thread count varying between 28 to 35 threads to the inch and in the requirements given with each design I give the amount of linen required to stitch the design in these thread counts and the appropriate threads to use with the different linens. I really recommend the use of finer linens as it means you can use the finer threads and a more delicate and lacy effect is achieved. Surprisingly it is also easier to hide the beginnings and endings of your threads.

For some projects I give the amount of linen required for a lower thread count 19 - 25 threads to the inch and these projects would be particularly suitable for beginners to this type of embroidery or for those who wish to create a bigger version of the design. A linen with a thread count of only 19 threads to the inch will make a much bigger design than linen with a thread count of 28 when stitched following the same pattern. The beauty of this embroidery is not lost when worked on a larger scale. Experiment and find a linen with a thread count that you find easy to work with, day or night.

It is important that the linen used has a nice open weave so that it is easy to see the 'holes' when you are stitching these designs.

Threads

The threads that we recommend for use with each design are given in the table at the start of the design instructions. In the table we give the threads to use with the different weights of linen. We also give a variety of threads that could be used so that you will be able to go to your local store, wherever it is, and buy one of the products we have listed or if that is not possible use our recommendations as a guide and buy an alternative product.

Threads available vary from store to store and country to country. I order my supplies from North America and Britain as well as buying locally and feel confident to recommend alternative threads for your use that I know will give you the end result you are seeking although they may be different from those generally available in New Zealand.

GENERAL NOTES

Traditionally the working thread should be about the same thickness as the individual threads of the fabric. A slightly finer thread gives a more delicate appearance which I tend to favour. The thread needs to be strong to maintain the tension and to withstand the pulling and to be sufficiently twisted not to fluff.

'Fine Thread'

In the text I refer to 'fine thread', this is used as a general term to apply to thread the weight and appearance of sewing cotton but either 100% cotton, silk or linen which is chosen to match the fabric. I give a number of alternatives to use and I know that the alternatives suggested will work well as I have used them all in my stitching at different times. Sometimes I will use a fine thread and work each stitch twice because of the 'precise' look which I feel this gives to my embroidery. Where I do this it is clearly advised in the text and an alternative thread is recommended if you would prefer to work each stitch only once. DMC Perle 12 is usually the alternative thread recommended for working four sided stitch, it is good to stitch with and avoids the need to work each stitch twice. It is also a good thread to use when you are not wanting a strong contrast between the satin and four sided stitches or when you want the four sided stitching to be more obvious.

Linen threads have also been used in some of the designs. These threads are ideal for use on linen fabric. This is the type of thread that would have been used historically. Linen thread is not mercerised so does not have a sheen but it is a good strong thread and nice to work with.

Stranded Silks and Cottons

I usually work satin stitch in a slightly heavier thread than I have used for the pulled work stitches, e.g. where as I use a fine cotton, silk or linen thread for working four sided stitch - I use two threads of stranded cotton or silk for satin stitch. I love all fabric and threads and have a wide variety of stranded silks and cotton threads. I use Madeira, DMC, Au Ver a Soie, Kreinik threads and Waterlilies by Caron and chose them by whichever has the exact shade that I want. They are all good to use and give the beauty and sheen that is wanted in this type of embroidery.

I use either two strands of silk or one strand of silk and one of stranded cotton. I rather like Waterlilies thread and when I use this I use one thread of variegated with one thread that matches the material using either silk or cotton stranded - whichever is the best match. Alternatively I may use one thread of variegated and different shades taken from the variegated thread if I wish to create highlights.

Stranded Silk thread may sometimes untwist and bulk up as it is stitched. Because it is also a thicker thread than stranded cotton one of each type of thread stitched together works well. You get the advantage of some sheen as well as a good cover.

Silk thread creates a beautiful sheen but does 'catch' on rough skin so try to handle the silk as little as possible. Move the needle along the thread frequently but remember to place the thread in the centre of the eye of the needle before moving it!

Separating threads

To ensure the threads lie nicely when stitched cut a length, then take the two threads you plan to use, separate them, then put them back together both lying in the same direction. You will find they will lie beautifully. However after saying this they do not have to lie in the same direction to achieve a smooth finish! I frequently use the 'loop' method for starting (page 11) when using silk thread and a smooth finish is still achieved despite the two threads running in opposite directions.

Colour in Satin Stitch

When introducing colour into your pulled thread embroidery. I recommend choosing colours from the 'light to medium' range if you wish the colours in your embroidery to blend subtly. The use of colour is unnecessary, the variety of stitches give contrast and colour only distracts the eye from the beauty of the stitching but with all the beautiful dyed threads available it is a shame not to experiment and use them a little.

Numbers in Threads

The higher the number the finer the thread. This applies to all threads, for example Perle 8 is thicker than Perle 12, Coton a broder 16 is thicker than Coton a broder 25.
Sometimes threads are referred to by two numbers such as Londonderry linen 80/3 or Au Ver a Soie 100/3. The first number of the pair refers to the relative diameter of the finished thread. The second to the number of single threads twisted together to make the thread. Again the higher the number the finer the thread.

Long Term Care of your Embroidery

When such a lot of time and effort has been put into a piece of embroidery its long term care is important.

- Put lukewarm water in your sink or basin with a little neutral soap to dissolve any body grease on your work. Immerse your embroidery in the water ensuring that it is completely wet.
- Rinse thoroughly in lots of lukewarm water until the water is absolutely clear.
- Lay your embroidery between two layers of toweling or roll it up in a towel and press out excess water. Do not crush, fold or wring!
- Pull gently working around all the sides to ensure your embroidery is the correct shape.
- Place the embroidery face down on several layers of sheeting and iron dry.
- Dry in the shade if it is large.
- If you have any queries, check with your local retailer who will know the different requirements for your area.

If your embroidery cannot be washed a firm iron on the wrong side with a damp cloth can be very effective in 'freshening' the appearance of your embroidery.

When embroidering work that can not be washed remember to wash your hands every time before starting to stitch. Place tissue paper over the work and only leave open a small area to stitch.

FROM MY HANDS

Stitches
General

The stitches used in this book are an introduction to some of the many stitches that can be used in Pulled Thread embroidery.

Most of the designs use counted satin stitch combined with four sided stitch, eyelets and more. Traditionally geometric or counted satin stitch has been combined with pulled thread embroidery in many different cultures over many years. By changing the angle of the stitches a play of light and shade can be obtained which adds to the charm of this embroidery.

I hope that the use of counted satin stitch will encourage those who have not used this technique before to try it! We all feel quite confident counting threads so counted satin stitch is a technique we can relax with. Four sided stitch is a most attractive stitch to use with counted satin stitch as it creates texture to offset the richness of the satin stitch whilst the eyelets give a light 'airy' look to the work.

No threads are pulled out in this stitching so it is not scary!

I find it is best if these stitches are worked in a hoop. The fabric is NOT drum tight in the hoop, rather it is held so that you can stitch with a sewing motion, not a stabbing motion. (See photograph page 52 which shows my work as I hold it in a hoop.) All the stitches are worked using a tapestry needle.

Most, not all, of these stitches are worked (if you are right handed) from right to left. The advantage of this is that the working thread stays on the right hand side, out of the way. Hold the work so that you are working towards yourself, rotating your work as you move around the different designs.

When I am stitching an 'all over' design for example Louisa's Opal page 53 I start stitching at the centre and work out. When I am working a border design for example the Danish Handkerchief page 51 I start at the corner.

Fig 1.

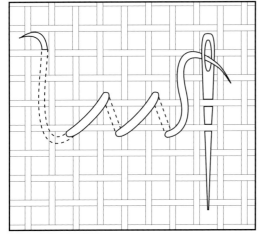

Starting *and* Finishing

Starting

There are a number of different ways of starting your thread. I personally favour leaving a 2 - 3 cm length of thread which I hold under my stitching, catching it in as I go.

If you are a beginner you may find it easier to leave a length of thread on the surface of the material to be finished later. To do this take your needle from the front to the back of the work approximately 5 cm away from where you plan to start stitching, leaving a 5 cm

STITCHES

length of thread on top of the fabric. Start to stitch and when you have covered some distance the thread on top of your work is taken to the back and finished into your stitching (Fig 1).

When you are working satin stitch you can work a couple of little back stitches in an area that will later be covered by the satin stitch.

Long Thread Method - Another 'trick' is to use an extra long thread. Start stitching with half the length of thread, use up all the thread working one way, then rethread your needle with the remaining length of thread, turn your work around and work in the other direction. This is particularly useful for satin and four sided stitch and when you start in a corner as it means there is no extra bulk in the corner (Fig 2).

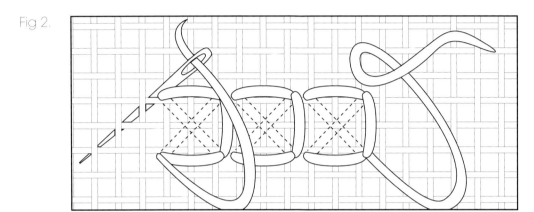

Fig 2.

Loop Method – Very useful when you are using a double thread. Take one long length of thread, fold in half and thread the cut ends through the eye of the needle. Start stitching in the correct position as shown on the chart, taking the needle under one thread, then thread the needle through the loop, now stitch the design following the chart. Neat and quick with not a knot in sight! (Fig 3).

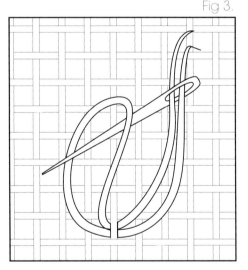

Fig 3.

Finishing

At the back of your work take the needle under your stitching for about 2 cms (3/4 of an inch), do a little slip or half knot then thread the needle back the 2 cms again and cut.

An invisible finishing technique which I like is to darn into the weave of the fabric. To do this I take my needle under the thread as shown - check on the front and you cannot see a thing! I only take my needle under two or three threads (Fig 4).

Where no specific instructions are given for starting and finishing at the start and end of stitches it is presumed you will use one of the methods given above.

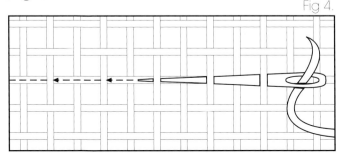

Fig 4.

Counted Satin Stitch *also known as* Geometric satin stitch

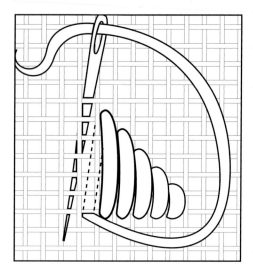

when pulled tightly called Pulled Satin
when worked individually straight stitch or flat stitch

This is a stitch with lots of possibilities! The basic satin stitch dates back to ancient times and many variations of the stitch have developed over the centuries.

Satin stitch is used to give solidity against lacy areas and shine against matt areas. It is the foil which 'lights' up the embroidery. The smooth beauty of this simple stitch compliments the other textured stitches.

I work the satin stitch in my embroidery in a heavier thread than I have used for the pulled work stitches, e.g. whereas I use a fine cotton, linen or silk thread for working four sided stitch - I use two threads of stranded cotton or silk for satin stitch. *The stitches should lie adjacent to each other without overlapping.* The thread should be kept evenly twisted throughout the work by turning the needle in the fingers when necessary. Each stitch should lie flat on the fabric and should not 'pull' the threads out of position. It is stitched using a tapestry needle.

To Start

Satin stitch is usually worked in blocks and this makes it very easy to start - just work a couple of little back stitches in an area that will later be covered by the satin stitch or use the Loop or Long Thread Methods (page 11).

To Finish

Take your needle through to the back of your work, slip it under the stitching for a short distance, do a little slip knot and then take the needle under the stitching for a further distance.

To work the Satin Stitch Stars

The satin stitch is best worked from the centre out. Work one section of the star - from the centre to the outer point, then take your thread under the threads at the back of the work back to the centre ready to stitch the next section of the star. Continue in this way until the star is completed.

Stem stitch

This stitch is also a very old stitch and used in many different types of embroidery, counted and surface. In Pulled Thread embroidery it is worked over a set number of threads and the number ties in with the other stitching on the embroidery. For example if four sided stitch is worked over four threads in your embroidery then the stem stitch will be worked over eight threads, going forward eight back four. This will ensure the different stitches tie in with each other well. It is worked using a tapestry needle.

This stitch can be worked with the thread below and to the right of the needle when it is called stem stitch or to the left of the needle when it is called outline stitch.

STITCHES

1. Start the thread in your preferred method. To begin working stem stitch bring your needle up in the correct position take one stitch over four threads (fig. 1).

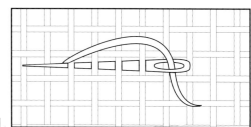
Fig 1.

2. Take the next stitch forward eight threads then bring the needle back four threads (fig. 2). Repeat this step the distance required.

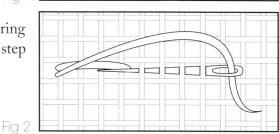
Fig 2.

Points and Turning –
To turn a corner complete the stitch then take your needle to the back of the work at the point, take your needle under the second to last stitch - this locks the stitch – then return the needle to the front in the correct position and start at Step 1.

Eyelets

The value of eyelets cannot be stressed too greatly. When placed individually they give a light and airy appearance to your embroidery and when grouped they create a lacy effect. They contrast nicely with the satin stitch. The object of an eyelet is to see the hole or space it has created not to see the surrounding stitches. These must be as insignificant as possible and a perfect round shape with no overlapping stitching.

The tension of the stitching must be firm and even so the holes in the eyelets are all the same size. **Bring the needle (tapestry) up in the outer edge and take it down through the centre for all variations of this stitch.** This enables you to pull the thread away from the centre.

To start all single eyelets hold the thread with a finger on the wrong side under the stitching and catch it as you move around - a knack soon acquired when stitching lots of these!

To finish at the back of the work thread the needle under the worked stitches and cut thread.
If it is being worked in a border or close to other stitching the thread can be carried from one to the next by slipping the thread under the stitches at the back of the work.

Refer to the charts accompanying each project for the way each eyelet is worked and the number of threads it is worked over. Square eyelets are worked in Danish Christmas page 72 but circular eyelets are more commonly used in the embroideries in this book.

All even numbers are in the centre

Fig 1

Square Eyelet
Always start at the outside of the eyelet and take the needle down in the centre. Work around in sequence following the diagram (fig. 1). I find it easier to start in the corner.

FROM MY HANDS

Circular Eyelet

In the embroidery in this book these eyelets are fine and delicate. They are stitched using a fine cotton, linen or silk thread (sewing cotton, or one thread of stranded cotton or silk can also be used) so that the eyelet creates a highlight in the embroidery.

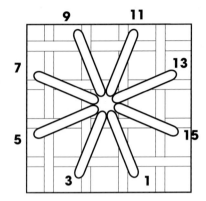

To create a nice shape, give a gentle push with a stiletto or similar tool, into the centre to start the eyelet but do not make the hole so big that the thread count is lost. On completion, another gentle push with the stiletto rounds it nicely and 'sets' the stitching. This gives a lovely circular eyelet with a fine edge. Work around the eyelets in sequence following the diagram (fig. 2). Note *there are no stitches on the straight* in this eyelet. Each eyelet is complete in itself.

Fig 2. All even numbers are in the centre

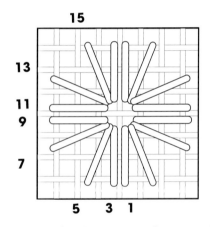

Eyelet with Central Cross

Eyelets can also be worked with variations. Leaving one thread at the centre of the eyelet gives an interesting look to the eyelet and is a rather eye catching alternative.

Start with a straight stitch, work in the order given following the chart (fig. 3).

Fig 3. All even numbers are in the centre

Handy Hint Neaten beginning and finishing threads by threading a sharp needle and taking the threads, on the wrong side, underneath the stitching in the completed eyelet. Finish one thread clockwise round the eyelet and the other anticlockwise.

Smyrna Stitch - *Double Cross*

Also known as leviathan stitch

Two cross stitches are worked one on top of the other. Work the first cross stitch on the diagonal as usual, (fig. 1). The second cross stitch is worked vertically over the top (fig. 2). In this work it is stitched using a tapestry needle.

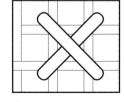
Fig 1.

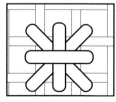
Fig 2.

STITCHES

Holbein Stitch

Also known as double running, line stitch, two sided line stitch plus more!

Holbein stitch is a very old stitch, made famous by the paintings of Hans Holbein a portrait painter of the sixteenth century. He is best known for his portraits of the royal family, Henry VIII and his children, in which this stitch was used in decoration on shirt collars, sleeves, and cuffs.

Holbein stitch is worked in running stitch in two journeys using a tapestry needle. It is important to keep the thread tension even. The first journey the stitches are evenly spaced leaving gaps to be filled in on the return journey (fig. 1).

There are different methods you can choose for working the return journey but the method I find most satisfactory is to bring my needle up through the fabric above the thread of the first journey and to go down below it (fig. 2).

After adjusting the thread tension your stitches will line up as shown (fig. 3).

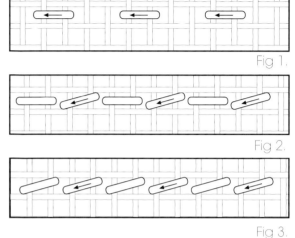

Fig 1.

Fig 2.

Fig 3.

Edging Stitches *and* Techniques

Hem Stitch, *Handkerchief*

This method of hem stitching is usually used to secure a hem or give a firm edge after one or two threads (or number required) have been withdrawn. Stitch using a fine tapestry needle to avoid splitting the threads. The number of threads to be withdrawn varies according to the fabric used and type of work. On very fine fabrics only a few threads are withdrawn whilst more threads must be withdrawn for wide borders suitable for sheets and tablecloths.

This stitch is one of the few that is worked from left to right.

Bring the needle through two threads down from the withdrawn threads (fig. 1). Take the needle to the right and pass it behind three to five threads pulling them together. Now take the needle two threads down at the back of the fabric and bring it through to the front ready to start your next stitch (fig. 2).

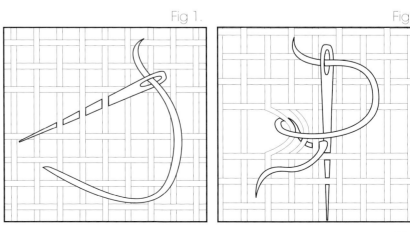

Fig 1.

Fig 2.

Nun's Stitch

Nun's stitch is an extremely useful narrow edging stitch. It is a very flat stitch making it ideal for bookmarks, needlebook pages etc. Working from right to left each stitch is worked twice. It is usually worked using a fine cotton, silk or linen thread.

1. Starting in your preferred method, bring the needle out three threads *below the point where surplus fabric is to be cut away* and take one stitch over three threads as shown with the needle going down into the fabric at the point where the surplus fabric is to be cut away (fig 1).

2. Take a second vertical stitch but change the direction of the needle and bring it out three threads down and to the left (fig. 2). This makes a diagonal stitch on the back of the fabric.

3. Work one horizontal stitch over three threads taking the needle down into the same hole that the earlier stitches went into (fig. 3).

4. Take a second horizontal stitch on top of the first (fig. 4).

5. Now take the needle back to a vertical position, up three threads and work the next stitch (fig 5). (The needle goes down at the point where surplus fabric is to be cut away.)

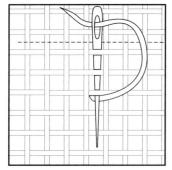
Fig 1.

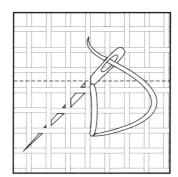
Fig 2.

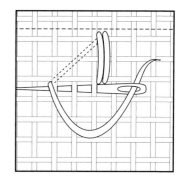
Fig 3.

Continue stitching in this manner. Turning a corner is easy, work the two horizontal stitches then bring the needle out directly below the right hand end of the last stitch, three threads down (fig. 6).

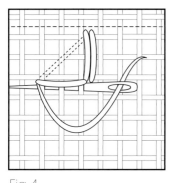
Fig 4.

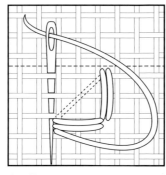
Fig 5.

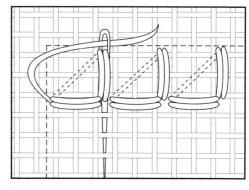
Fig 6.

STITCHES

Four sided *stitch*

Four sided stitch provides texture and interest, the contrast to satin stitch. It is one of the most frequently used stitches in pulled thread embroidery and often forms the basis or outline of the design. The lines can be worked horizontally, vertically or on the diagonal. It should be worked with an even tension causing no distortion of the fabric.

Use a fine tapestry needle and fine cotton, linen or silk thread (sewing machine thread can also be used). Sometimes I work each stitch twice with fine thread, to achieve the very clean 'precise' look that I like. Alternatively you can use a slightly heavier thread and work each stitch only once.

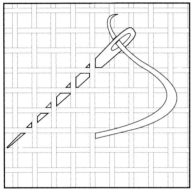

Perle 12 is good when you are not wanting a strong contrast between the satin and four sided stitches. In the designs I give the threads to use for either option.

Although it is made up of four separate stitches, one on each side of the square one complete square is called 'one four sided stitch'.

Four sided stitch is worked in horizontal rows, *always moving from right to left*. Follow figs 1-4 pulling each stitch firmly as you work. Repeat this sequence until the row is complete.

Fig. 1

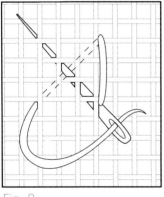 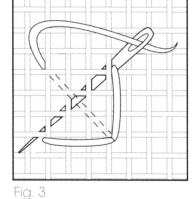 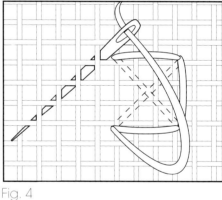

Fig. 2 Fig. 3 Fig. 4

To turn a corner see figs 5 & 6. Stop one stitch before the corner, take the first stitch, then turn your fabric and continue working from right to left in the usual manner.

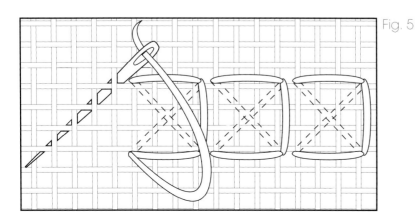

Fig. 5

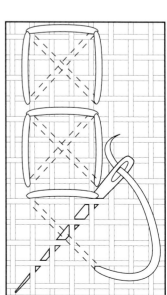

Fig. 6

17

FROM MY HANDS

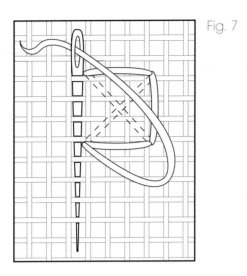
Fig. 7

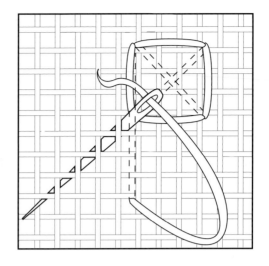
Fig. 8

To work on the diagonal see figs 7 & 8. Work the fourth stitch to complete the square but bring your needle out four threads below the square. When you work your next stitch make sure you catch it round the long stitch at the back of the work. (You can actually feel the thread so it is easy to catch in.) Complete square in usual way.

To work in rows – complete the stitch at the end of the row, turn your embroidery so that you are still working right to left, take the needle along at the back of your work to the right position to continue.

Scandanavian Edging *Stitch*

This is a light but very durable edging, simple to do but most effective. This stitch is actually two stitches worked in two separate stages. The first is stem stitch which is worked on **the wrong side of the fabric** using a heavier thread to create a nice textured edge, then an edging stitch is worked.

Stem stitch

I have found after using many different weights of thread, that a Perle 8 thread is perfect for material with 25 to 30 threads to the inch, for finer fabric (32 – 36 threads per inch) Perle 12 is better. It is important to create a big enough 'picot' to be seen as part of the edging and yet be fine enough to enable you to work the second row of stitching comfortably. If the thread is too fine the 'picot' will disappear into the fabric and be lost between the stitches.

If you have been working four sided stitch over three or four threads elsewhere on your embroidery then the stem stitch will also be worked over the same number of threads - this will mean that the rows of stitching will all line up. To learn, work over four threads.

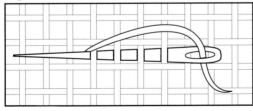
Fig 1.

1. Start in your preferred starting method and begin the first row of stitching - the stem stitch, *working on the wrong side* of the fabric. Bring your needle up in the correct position take one stitch over four threads (fig. 1). Work from left to right.

STITCHES

2. Take the next stitch forward eight threads then bring the needle back four threads (fig. 2).

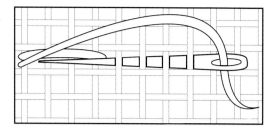

Fig 2.

3. Take a second stitch over the last four threads (fig. 3) - repeat steps 2 & 3 for the length required.

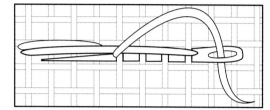

Fig 3.

To turn a corner

When you have worked the second stitch over four threads (step 3) take the needle along four threads from the end stitch and bring it back along and up at the corner (fig. 4). This will give you a diagonal stitch on the surface of the material but this is the wrong side of the material so it will be hidden in the next row of stitching. Work one stitch over the four threads, now continue steps 2 & 3 till the next corner!

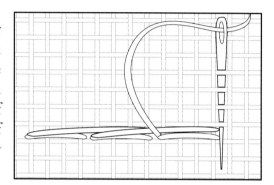

Fig 4.

When you have completed the stem stitch, turn your work to the right side and fold the fabric along the line of stem stitches with the stitches creating little 'picots' on the edge of the fold.

Edging Stitch

This is worked on the right side of the fabric over four threads each way. With a new thread bring your needle out four threads beneath the 'picots' and work two horizontal stitches over the same four threads (fig. 5). It is important the stitches are worked directly beneath the 'picots'.

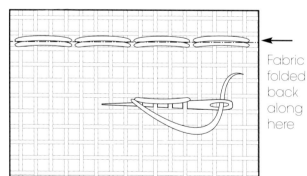

Fig 5.

Next work two vertical stitches. When you work the second one take your needle four threads along ready to work the next two horizontal stitches (fig. 6). Continue in this way until you come to the corner.

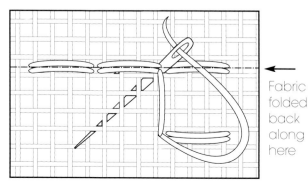

Fig 6.

FROM MY HANDS

> **Handy Hint** - To make it easier to work the edging stitch I withdraw a thread. For example if I am working my edging stitch over four threads I will withdraw the fifth thread down creating a bigger 'gap' for the needle to slip into ensuring all my stitches are placed correctly.

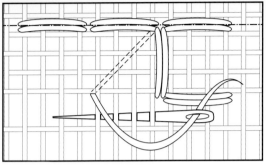

Fig 7.

Withdraw one thread to create a bigger gap to stitch in

Withdraw a second thread to create a channel to cut in

Trim fabric back, after the edging stitch has been worked, to one thread below the stitching, only trim 5 - 7 cm at a time. As a guide for cutting pull out one thread to create a channel to cut along (Fig 7).

To work round the Corner

When you are two stitches from the corner work the two horizontal stitches - the first part of the next stitch. Stop. Trim the excess fabric away to the outer edge of the fabric (use the withdrawn thread as a cutting guide). Now fold back the fabric along the stem stitched line - it will create a nice sharp point - and work three vertical stitches through all the layers of fabric. Now work three more stitches on the other side of the corner (fig. 8). Continue stitching in the usual manner.

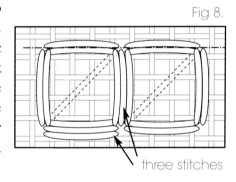

Fig 8.

three stitches

Reverse Chain Stitch and *Chain Stitch Joining*

This is a most useful, and slightly different way of joining pincushions, sachets etc together. Chain stitch along the edge of the item to be joined. I usually make each chain stitch as long as the four sided stitch beside it, or twice the length if that seems more appropriate. The diagrams show it worked over three threads.

If it is not beside four sided stitch link the length of the chain stitches to the work already stitched so that you get a uniform size for each stitch.

I prefer to work Reverse Chain stitch as it is easier to count the number of threads you are covering when you work it this way. *When I use it in these designs it is used to create an edge to be joined and whipped for this reason I start and do the corners a little differently.*

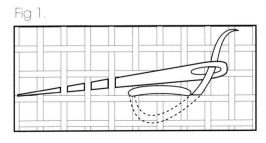

Fig 1.

Bring your needle out at the corner and start with a small running stitch over three threads. Then bring your needle back out at the corner and take a second running stitch over the same three threads but this time bring the needle forward three threads, (fig. 1).

STITCHES

Now take the needle back under the two running stitches (under the stitches don't catch the fabric) then bring it forward and take it down at the same point it was brought to the surface. Bring the needle forward a further three threads ready to start the next stitch (fig. 2).

Continue in this manner (fig. 3).

Fig 2.

Fig 3.

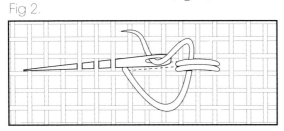
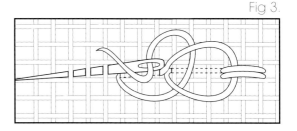

The way I do the corners makes a very nice sharp corner as well as a very 'firm' corner. To turn a corner take the thread down in the usual position but bring it out three threads along (fig. 4). Now work two back stitches over the three threads, (they almost look like a chain stitch but are more stable). With the second back stitch bring your needle forward three threads and continue as normal (fig. 5).

Fig 4.

Fig 5.

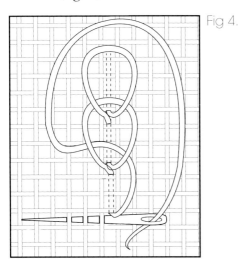
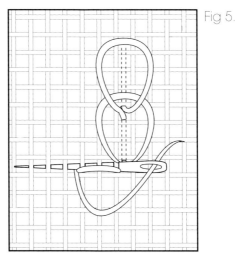

To finish bring your needle out in the usual position, this will be in the same hole that your initial running stitches were worked in. Take your needle back round the preceding chain as usual, then down where it came out, (fig. 6). Finish thread off in your preferred method.

Work this chain stitch edge along both pieces of fabric to be joined. Fold the excess fabric back so the chains are right on the edge of the fabric, bring a needle out near a corner, holding the two pieces together with right sides facing out, join the two chain stitch borders by whipping both chain stitches together (fig. 7).

Fig 7. Folded two edges lined up

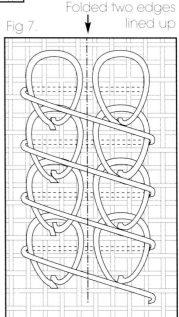

Fig 6.

FROM MY HANDS

Bookmarks
finished size 5 x 20 cms (2 x 8 in)

Bookmarks are a lovely gift for yourself or someone special! They are quite quickly made yet different stitches and techniques are acquired which are used again in later designs. The fine edging stitch used means the bookmarks will not damage your book's binding and will grace the bedside table where they are placed.

These are a good introduction to working with good quality linen, using fine thread for the nun's stitch edging and stranded cotton or silk for the satin stitch design. Beautiful fabrics are a special joy to work with and the combination of satin stitch with pulled thread stitches is very effective. If you are a beginner you may prefer to use a linen with a lower thread count. Check what is available at your local shop and choose a linen you like the look of and with a thread count you feel comfortable with. Threads to use with the different weights of linen are given in the table.

I make these four or five at a time stitching the outline first, often when I am watching television and then I pick the fillings from designs that appeal to me. Just leave two to three threads between each one so that they can be cut apart easily (leave 5 cm, (2 in) extra at each end for the fringe). I have given five different designs, try these then try any design that appeals to you.

I think they are fun to make and hope you do too!

Stitches used: nun's stitch, four sided stitch, satin and eyelets

In these patterns the nun's and four sided stitch is worked over three threads

Materials

- Exact details of fabric and threads used are given here in italics as a guide. I tend to make more than one of these at once so would buy
- a piece of linen approximately 30 x 40 cm.
- 'Fine thread*' this is used as a general term to apply to thread the weight and appearance of sewing cotton but either 100% cotton, silk or linen which is chosen to match the fabric, a selection of suitable threads is given in the table.
- Stranded cotton or silk for the satin stitch
- Tapestry Needle Size 24 or 26

BOOKMARKS

Instructions

Neaten the raw edges of your fabric.
Cut a 35 - 40 cm length of 'fine thread'* then start to work nun's stitch about 5 cm (2in) up from the bottom and 1 cm (1/2in) from the side of the linen. Nun's stitch is worked over three threads (see page 16 for nun's stitch). Stitch about 20 cm (8in) for the length of the book mark then turn and work approximately 5 cm (2 in) across the top.

Bookmarks

linen	'fine thread*'	matching stranded cotton or silk
quantity required 30 x 40 cm	threads used for nun's stitch	threads used for counted satin stitch four sided stitch and eyelets
25 - 36 threads to the inch **30 *Vanilla Gold Legacy Linen***	• **Londonderry Linen Thread Maple Sugar 80/3** • Zwicky 100% cotton or silk • Guterman 100 % silk or cotton • Au Ver a Soie 100/3 100% silk • Madeira Cotona • Dewhurst Sylko • DMC Dentelles 80 for fabric with 19 – 30 threads per inch	two threads **D** 3047, 918 **AvD** 3732, 2636 **M** 2205, 0314 **A** 886, 351
19 threads to the inch	DMC Perle 12, Coton a broder 25	Use three threads for satin stitch on linen 19 – 25 threads to in inch.

D = DMC **AvD** = Au Ver a Soie D'Alger **M** = Madeira **A** = Anchor

• The availability of threads varies around the world. We give alternatives which we know will give equal satisfaction in their use and create an equally beautiful design for you.

• Materials used shown in italics.

Work an uneven number of nun's stitches so that the designs are easy to centre. Complete the second side and base of the book mark before working the satin stitch filling. Full instructions for starting and finishing threads are given on page 10.

Diamond *Bookmark*

Chart A

Fold the book mark in half in both directions then tack under and over three threads to mark the centre. Start at the centre and work the diamond using two threads of stranded cotton or silk. The first stitch is worked over two threads, follow the chart from this point.

It is easier to stitch this design if you work the diamond, then one side of the box, the next diamond, etc until you are about 6-8 threads from the nun's stitch outline. Stop. To work back up slide the needle under the diamond, work the other side of the box, slide you needle under the next diamond up to the next box. Continue in this way.

Each line represents one thread

CHART A
— cross line indicates end of each stitch

Zig Zag *Bookmark*

Chart B

Stitch the centre zig zag using two threads of stranded cotton or silk and working from right to left, starting at the top of the chart and three threads from one end of your bookmark. The triangles are completed one side at a time. As each triangle is finished, slip the thread through the bottom three stitches at the base of the zig zag between each triangle to take the working thread to the correct position for starting the next triangle.

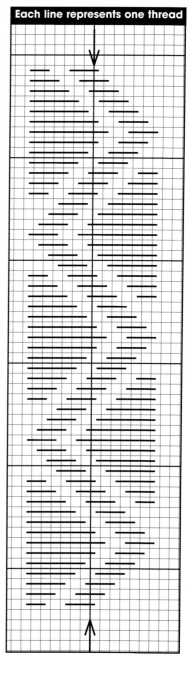

CHART B
Each line represents one thread

BOOKMARKS

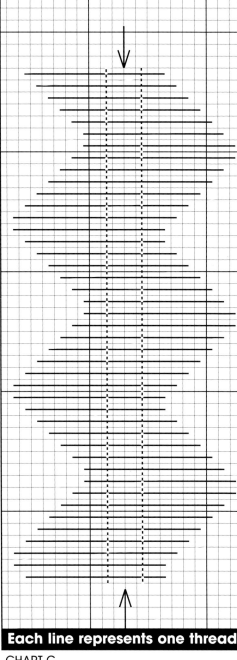

CHART C
••• dotted line indicates
end of each stitch

Triangle *Bookmark*
Chart C

This bookmark is stitched using two threads of stranded cotton or silk, working from right to left and starting at one end. Count the nun's stitches across the bottom and find the centre three threads. Come up 1 cm (1/2in) from the lower edge of nun's stitch and work the central row of satin stitch over three threads until 1 cm (1/2in) from the other end. Now work the zigzag along one side of the satin stitch. It is worked over two threads increasing to eight threads. Follow the chart and when you have completed one side, turn your work and stitch the other side to complete.

Corinthian Bookmark
Chart D

Using two threads of stranded cotton or silk start the satin stitch in the centre. Work from right to left, when you have reached one end, finish off. Go back to the centre, turn the work around and stitch to the other end.

Using one thread of stranded cotton or silk, work four sided stitch on both sides of the centre pattern, starting one thread out from the edge of the central design.

Eyelet *Bookmark*
Chart E

Using two threads of stranded cotton or silk start satin stitching at one end, working from right to left. The first four stitches are over six threads then reduce to three threads for the eyelet. Work following the chart and complete the satin stitch on one side before stitching the second.

Using one thread of stranded cotton or silk, work four sided stitch on both sides of the centre design, starting one thread out from the edge of the central design. With the same thread work the eyelets. Complete each eyelet, following the chart, then slide the needle through the satin stitch down to the correct position to start the next eyelet.

To Trim all Bookmarks

When you have completed the stitching cut excess fabric away from the long edges of your bookmark. Pull out one thread just beyond your stitching to create a channel to cut in. Take great care not to cut any of the stitching. Cut approximately 5cm (2in) extra top and bottom and pull the threads away to make a fringe.

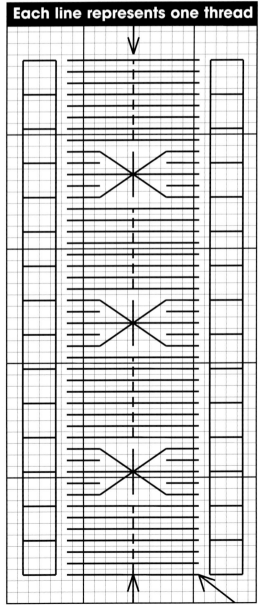

CHART E
---dotted line indicates end of each stitch

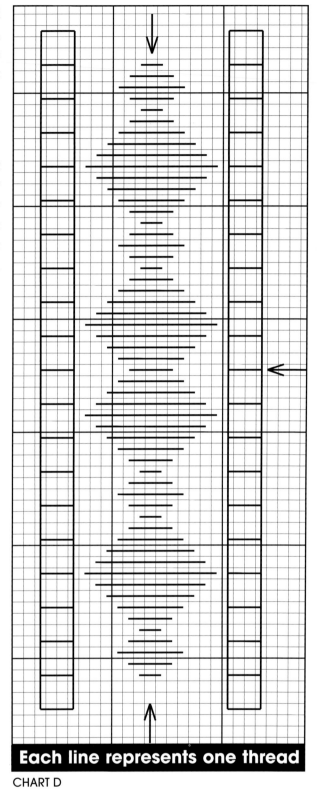

CHART D

Pink Simplicity
Finished size 16 x 24 cms (6 x 9in)

A dainty design that is stitched using fine silk thread and worked on a fine fabric makes a combination that is hard to resist! This is a delightfully flexible design - we show it worked on fabric with 32 threads to the inch, but it looks equally attractive worked on a linen with a lower thread count.

Not only can this design be worked on many different weights of linen it can also be worked any size that you like - from a coaster to a tablecloth! The pattern repeat is marked on the chart so that it is easy to alter the size of the mat to suit your requirements.

If you would like to just try out a little project using this dainty design, the Lavender Bag is for you. Pretty and useful, these feature just one star motif, see page 32. Large or small this is a delightful design to stitch.

Stitches used: four sided, satin, eyelet and Scandanavian four sided edging

In this design the four sided and Scandanavian edging stitches are worked over four threads, the satin stitch is worked over two threads

It is recommended that you stitch the design in the sequence given

Materials

- Select linen to suit your particular requirements, if you are new to this type of stitching use linen with a thread count that you feel comfortable with. The correct threads to use on linen with a thread count from 19 to 35 threads per inch are given in the table and all will create a most attractive design.
- 'Fine thread*' this is used as a general term to apply to thread the weight and appearance of sewing cotton but either 100% cotton, silk or linen which is chosen to match the fabric, see table. It is used for four sided stitch and the second stage of Scandanavian edging stitches and a selection of suitable threads is given in the table.
- Two threads of stranded cotton or silk are used in three different shades of pink for the stars. One thread is used for the eyelets.
- 15 cm embroidery hoop
- Tapestry Needle No. 24 or 26

FROM MY HANDS

Instructions

Neaten the raw edges of your linen.
All the four sided stitch is worked using 'fine thread' see table.

Thread your needle with 'fine thread' and start at the corner using the long thread method (see page 11). Come in about 2.5cm (1in)

Pink Simplicity

linen 'antique white' quantity required - numbers in bold equal threads per inch*	'fine thread*' threads for four sided stitch, 2nd part of Scandinavian edging stitch	matching stranded cotton or silk threads for counted satin stitch, eyelets, 1st part of Scandinavian edging stitch
36 25 x 30 cm (10 x 12 in) **32** 25 x 35 cm (10 x 14 in) **30** 30 x 40 cm (12 x 16 in)	• Zwicky 100% cotton or silk • Guterman 100 % silk or cotton • Au Ver a Soie 100/3 100% silk • Madeira Cotona • Dewhurst Sylko • Londonderry Linen Thread 80/3 • DMC Dentelles 80 for fabric with 19 – 30 threads per inch	D 3042, 3727, 224 AvD 4633, 4632, 4622 M 0807, 0809, 0813 A 870, 1016, 893
25 35 x 25 cm (15 x 20 in) **19** 45 x 60 cm (20 x 24 in)	• DMC Perle 12 • Coton a broder 25 • DMC Cordonnet 80 • Au Ver a Soie Perlee	use three threads of above colours for 19 & 25 count linen

D = DMC **Av** = Au Ver a Soie D'Alger **M** = Madeira **A** = Anchor

- The availability of threads varies around the world. We give alternatives which we know will give equal satisfaction in their use and create an equally beautiful design for you.
- Material used shown in italics.
- * Pink Simplicity has two corners and two pattern repeats along the short side and two corners and four pattern repeats on the long side. Each corner covers 80 threads, each pattern repeat covers 52 threads.

PINK SIMPLICITY

CHART A
start at corner

each satin stitch worked over two threads

...dotted lines indicate end of each stitch

each line represents one thread

from each edge of your linen and stitching from right to left work four sided stitch over four threads each way for a reasonable distance in each direction - at least enough to work the corner and one pattern repeat, preferably more! This is the foundation row and is a useful guide for the rest of your stitching. It is worked right round the edge of the design. (Scandanavian edging stitch will be worked beyond this.) For more information on four sided stitch see page 17.

Complete all the four sided stitch before working the satin stitch stars.

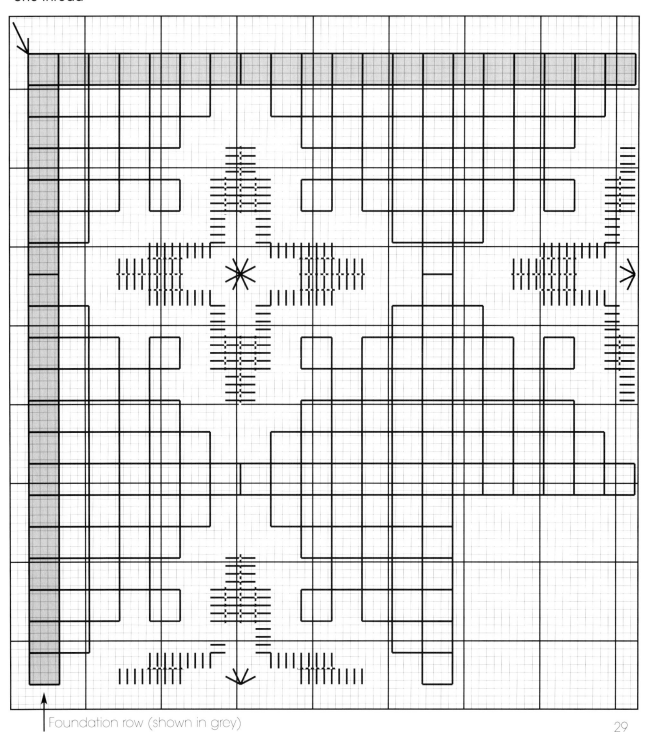

Foundation row (shown in grey)

FROM MY HANDS

Four Sided Stitch - Corner
Chart A

With your foundation row in place. Refer to Chart A and work the corner in four sided stitch. At the end of each row turn your work 180° so that you continue working from right to left. Note there is one 'floating' stitch which is easiest worked as a continuation of the row it connects with at the corner.

> **Handy Hint** - When stitching four sided stitch, to ensure you stitch in the right sequence remember, side, bottom, top side!

Four Sided Stitch - *Edges (Pattern Repeat)*
Chart B

Stitching from right to left, work four sided stitch following the pattern. Remember the outer row on the design is the foundation row and work in from here. Note there is a gap of two four sided stitches between each pattern repeat. Turn the work 180° at the end of each row so that you continue working in the correct manner. I find it easiest to complete one pattern repeat (working from the outside edge into the middle) before starting the next. This section of the pattern may be repeated until the mat is the desired size. Once again, note the 'floating' stitch.

Satin Stitch Stars

The stars are stitched in three different shades of pink, the placement of the colour is completely haphazard!
Start at the outer 'point' of the stars and position them by lining them up with the four sided stitch. Refer to Chart A for the 'star' pattern.

Using two threads of stranded cotton the colour of your choice, work the first line of nine satin stitches over two threads then turn your work around and work a second line of satin stitch over two threads. At the back of your work take the needle under your stitching to the correct position to work the next part of the star, continue stitching round the star in this way. See fig. 1

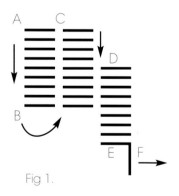

Fig 1.

Eyelets

These are 'circular' eyelets stitched using one thread of the stranded cotton in the same colour that you worked the star. Refer to Chart A for the pattern and page 14 for more information on working eyelets.

PINK SIMPLICITY

Scandanavian Edging Stitch

(For detailed instructions on worked this stitch see page 18.)

Using two strands of one of your pink threads work the first row of Scandanavian edging stitch, the stem stitch, *on the wrong side of your work*. It is positioned four threads beyond the foundation row of four sided stitch and is worked going forward over eight threads and back four threads each time. Start near the corner lining it up directly beneath the four sided stitch in the foundation row. Work the final row of stitching using the same thread you used for the four sided stitch.

Finished. I do hope you have found stitching this design satisfying and the end result a delight!

CHART B
each satin stitch worked over two threads

...dotted lines indicate end of each stitch

each line represents one thread

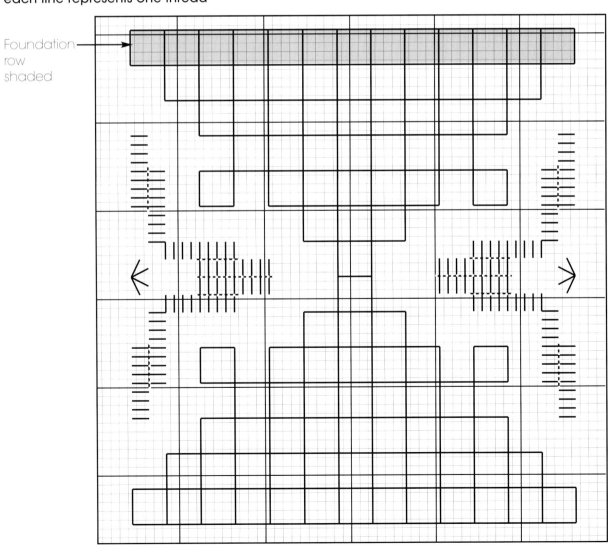

Foundation row shaded

FROM MY HANDS

Sweet Lavender Bag
finished size 10 x 15 cm (4 x 6 in)

Scented bags have been used for many centuries, to sweeten chests or drawers of clothing, to soothe the nerves and to induce a refreshing sleep. Different herbs have been used for the different purposes, but the more popular filling for these little bags nowadays is the strongly scented lavender.

This little bag has one star front and back surrounded by four sided stitch.

Stitches used: four sided, satin, hem, eyelet and Scandanavian edging stitch

In this pattern the four sided and Scandanavian edging stitches are worked over four threads, the satin stitch is worked over two threads

It is recommended that you stitch this in the sequence given

Materials

- This dainty lavender bag was stitched on 28 count, lavender coloured, linen.
- 'Fine thread*' this is used as a general term to apply to thread the weight and appearance of sewing cotton but either 100% cotton, silk or linen which is chosen to match the fabric, see table. It is used for four sided and hem stitches and the second part of Scandanavian edging stitch. A selection of suitable threads is given in the table.
- Two threads of stranded cotton were used for the pink star
- Matching Perle 8 was used for the first part of Scandanavian edging stitch
- Tapestry Needle No 24 or 26
- The drawstring is a handmade cord using two different shades of pink stranded cotton. A ribbon would be an attractive alternative.
- Tacking thread
- 15 cm embroidery hoop

Instructions

Neaten the raw edges of your linen.

Count in ten threads and then work the first row of Scandanavian edging stitch, the stem stitch, right round the edge of the linen and down the centre, outlining a shape approximately 21.5 cm (8 in)

LAVENDER BAGS

wide by 15 cm (6 in) high, (fig. 1). Remember the side you work this on will become the wrong side of the fabric. Use matching Perle 8 thread and work each stem stitch going forward eight threads and back four (For detailed information on Scandanavian edging stitch see page 18.).

Count down nine stitches, withdraw one thread, this will be used for the drawstring. (Ignore the missing thread when you work the

Sweet Lavender Bag

linen	'fine thread*'	matching stranded cotton or silk	
quantity required 20 x 30 cm (8 x 12 inches) for all linens	threads for four sided, hem stitch and eyelets, 2nd part of Scandinavian edging stitch	threads for counted satin stitch, two threads	threads for 1st part of Scandinavian edging stitch
28 - 36 threads per inch *fabric with 28 threads per inch was used*	• *Zwicky 100% cotton or silk* • Guterman 100 % silk or cotton • Au Ver a Soie 1003 100% silk • Madeira Cotona • Dewhurst Sylko • Londonderry Linen Thread 80/3 • DMC Dentelles 80 for fabric with 19 - 30 threads per inch	**D** 3042, 3727 **AvD** 4633, 4632 **M** 0807, 0809 **A** 870, 1016	**D** *Perle 8* **Av** Perlee **L** 50/3 Coton a broder 16
19 - 25 threads per inch	• DMC Perle 12 • Coton a broder 25 • Londonderry Linen Thread 30/3	three threads for satin stitch on linen with 19 - 25 threads to the inch.	**D** Perle 5 or 8 **L** 18/3

D = DMC **AvD** = Au Ver a Soie D'Alger **Kr** = Kreinik Mori **M** = Madeira **A** = Anchor **L** = Londonderry

• The availability of threads varies around the world. We give alternatives which we know will give equal satisfaction in their use and create an equally beautiful design for you.

• Material used shown in italics.

FROM MY HANDS

second row of Scandanavian edging stitch.) Work two rows of hem stitch, one on either side of the withdrawn thread using the 'fine thread'. (Refer to page 15 for hem stitch instructions)

Fold each side of the lavender bag in quarters and tack under and over four threads marking the centre in each direction.

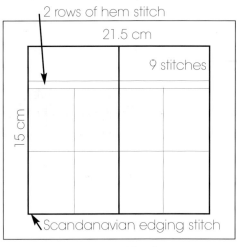

Fig. 1

Four Sided *Stitch*

Starting at the centre count out 28 threads (seven tacked stitches) to the right hand side and work one four sided stitch. It is worked using 'fine thread'. Four sided stitch is worked on the diagonal to form a diamond shape to enclose the star, see chart. Refer to page 18 for further information on working four sided stitch on the diagonal. Don't miss the 'floating' four sided stitch which comes in from the edge of the diamond.

Satin Stitch Stars

The star is stitched using two threads of stranded cotton or silk in a matching shade of pink. Start at the outer 'point' of the star and work the first line of nine satin stitches over two threads, then turn your work around 180° and work a second line of satin stitch over two threads. At the back of your work take the needle under your stitching to the correct position to work the next part of the star, continue stitching round the star in this way, (fig. 2.).

Refer to the Chart for its placement. An easy guide is to count in from the four sided stitch diamond.

Eyelets

This is a 'circular' eyelet stitched using one thread of the stranded cotton in the same colour that you worked the star. Follow the chart for its placement. For further information on stitching a 'circular' eyelet refer to page 14.

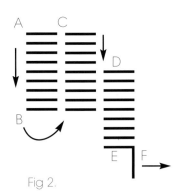

Fig 2.

The design is repeated on the reverse side of the bag.

To complete

Fold the top of the bag down along the line of stem stitch (the first row of Scandanavian edging stitch). Work the second row of Scandanavian edging stitch - along this edge. It is stitched using 'fine thread'. Trim excess material away with care! (Leave one thread, withdraw the next and cut in the channel.)

Now fold the bag in half down the centre line of stem stitch and work the edging stitch here starting at the top. When you near the lower edge trim the excess fabric back to about 1 cm (1/2 in) and

LAVENDER BAGS

Handy Hint
It is wise to leave the trimming until you are ready to sew to avoid excess fraying.

turn in all the fabric at the lower edge. (You need to leave enough to catch in the edging stitch across the base). Complete sewing to the lower edge.

Now work the second stage of Scandanavian edging stitch across the base and up the outside of the bag (tucking in remaining raw edges). Stitch firmly through all the layers of the material.

Turn the bag inside out and trim. (Leave one thread, withdraw the next and cut in the channel.) Make a cord or thread a ribbon between the hemstitching and your lavender bag is almost too pretty to fill with lavender!

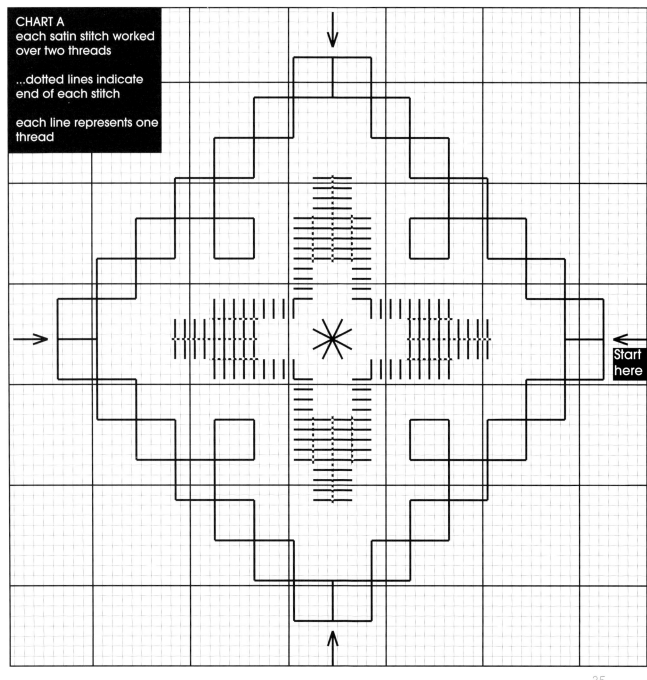

CHART A
each satin stitch worked over two threads

...dotted lines indicate end of each stitch

each line represents one thread

FROM MY HANDS

Danish Coaster
finished size 6 cm square

The design for this dainty coaster was taken directly from 'A Danish Handkerchief.' It has the geometric or counted satin stitch star surrounded by a four sided stitch diamond. These little coasters would be beautiful on the table with 'A Danish Handkerchief' but would also look most attractive on the table on their own. They are a good introduction to this embroidery. My coasters are stitched on linen with 35 threads to the inch. If you are just beginning, stitch these on linen with less threads to the inch. They will be easier to stitch and make larger coasters. Alternative fabrics and the threads to use with them are given in the table.

Stitches used: counted or geometric satin stitch, four sided stitch, Scandanavian edging stitch and circular eyelets

In this design the Scandanavian edging stitch and four sided stitch are worked over three threads

It is recommended that you stitch these in the sequence given

Materials

- 'Fine thread*' this is used as a general term to apply to thread the weight and appearance of sewing cotton but either 100% cotton, silk or linen which is chosen to match the fabric, see table. It is used for stitching the eyelets, four sided stitch and the second part of Scandanavian edging stitch. If a heavier thread is preferred Coton a broder 25 may be used, see 'Four sided stitch diamond'.
- Matching stranded cotton or silk is used for the satin stitching
- Matching Perle 12 for the first part of Scandanavian edging stitch
- Tapestry Needles Size 24 or 26
- Crewel needle which has a big eye but sharp point for starting and finishing threads.
- Contrast thread for tacking
- 15 cm embroidery hoop

Instructions

Neaten the raw edges of your linen.
Fold your fabric in half, then tack each side in half lengthways. Work all the four sided stitch on the Coasters before working the satin stitch or eyelets.
Stitch from right to left, holding your embroidery so that you are working towards yourself.

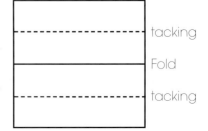
Fold, tack down centre of each half lengthways

DANISH COASTER

Four Sided Stitch Diamond

Measure in 2 cms (3/4 in) from the edge of the material and start working four sided stitch at the centre of one side of the coaster, see chart. I like to sew four sided stitch with fine cotton but to achieve the crisp, precise finish I like I work each stitch twice. Do not sew one four sided stitch and then go back and sew again on top of the

Danish Coasters

linen cream	'fine thread*'	matching stranded cotton or silk	
quantity required numbers in bold equal threads per inch	threads used for four sided stitch, eyelets, 2nd part of Scandinavian edging stitch	threads used for counted satin stitch	threads used for 1st part of Scandinavian edging stitch
Linen with 35 threads to the inch was used **32 - 35** 20 cm square (20 in sq) **28 - 30** 25 cm sq (10 in sq)	• Zwicky 100% cotton or silk • *Guterman 100 % silk or cotton* • Au Ver a Soie 1003 100% silk • Madeira Cotona • Dewhurst Sylko • Londonderry • DMC Dentelles 80 for fabric with 19 – 30 threads per inch	two threads used **D** Ecru **Av** F 1 **M** Ecru **A** 926 **Kr** Cream	**D** Perle 12 **Av** Perlee **Kr** Serica **L** 80/3
25 25 cm sq (10 in sq) **19** 35 cm sq (14 in sq)	• DMC Perle 12 • Coton a broder 25 • Londonderry linen thread 50/3	use three threads for satin stitch on fabric with 19 – 25 threads per inch	**D** Perle 5 or 8 **L** 30/3 **Kr** Serica

D = DMC **Av** = Au Ver a Soie D'Alger **Kr** = Kreinik Mori **M** = Madeira **A** = Anchor
L = Londonderry

- The availability of threads varies around the world. We give alternatives which we know will give equal satisfaction in their use and create a beautiful design for you.
- Materials used shown in italics.

first stitch as this will not give the correct tension, rather embroider each part of the stitch twice as you are working it. If you would rather not do this use Coton a broder 25 and then double stitching will not be required. (For more information on four sided stitch worked on the diagonal see page 18).

Satin Stitch *Stars*

Work the satin stitch star found in the centre of the diamond. To ensure correct placement of the star you may find it helpful to quickly run a further tacking thread over and under three threads from top to bottom of the diamond.

To stitch the satin stitch stars use two threads of stranded cotton or silk and refer to the Chart. Start at the centre of the star working one segment of the star at a time.

There are four threads not stitched at the centre of the satin stitch star. Put a pin in the diagonal across the four threads that form the central unstitched square. This will ensure that your first stitches are positioned correctly, later remove the pin.

The first stitch is over two threads and in the following rows, one side of the star is kept straight, whilst on the other side one more thread is picked up each line. At the eighth row this is reversed, the side that was straight now decreases one thread per line and the other side has a straight edge. When you have completed one segment of the star take your needle under the stitching at the back of your work to the centre ready to being the next segment. Complete the star.

Quarter Stars

Using two threads of stranded cotton work a quarter star in each corner. Refer to the chart for their placement.

Eyelets

The eyelets are worked using the fine cotton thread used for the four sided stitch or one thread of stranded cotton or silk. They are not stitched twice. All the eyelets in this embroidery are stitched with the centre of the eyelet lined up with the centre of the diamond four sided stitch outline and with the top of the fourth four sided stitch counting from the point. See the arrows on the Chart. Refer to page 14 for detailed information on stitching circular eyelets.

DANISH COASTER

Scandanavian Edging Stitch

Handy Hint
Try not to start new threads or new stitching right in a corner because the bulk of extra threads can make a corner look 'ungainly'.

The first line of this stitch, the stem stitch, is worked six threads beyond the line of four sided stitch *on the wrong side* of your embroidery. It is stitched using matching Perle 12 thread going forward six threads and coming back three. Line the stitching up directly beneath the four sided stitch and start near the centre of one side beneath the double four sided stitches, see chart. It is easier to count out from here.

The second journey of this stitch is worked using the fine linen, cotton or silk thread used in four sided stitch. For detailed information on working Scandanavian edging stitch refer to page 18.

This coaster is a beautiful example of geometric or counted satin stitch and pulled thread work.

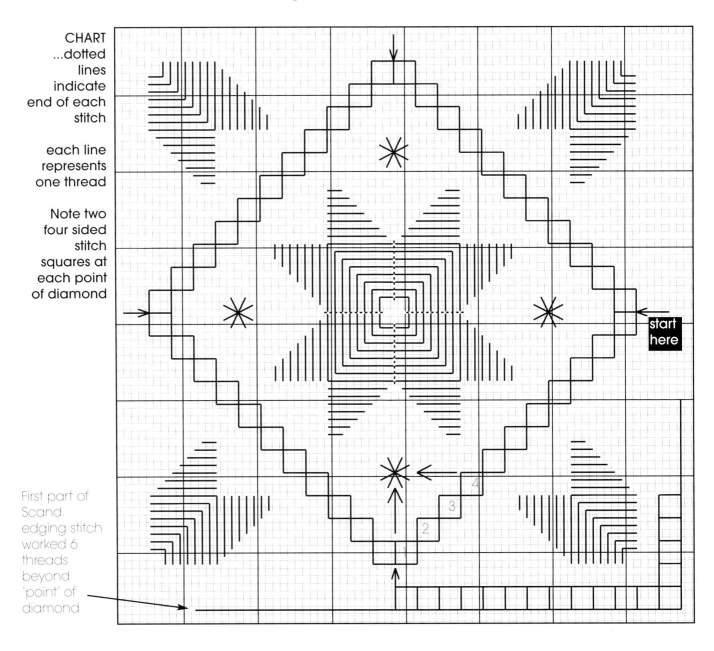

CHART ...dotted lines indicate end of each stitch

each line represents one thread

Note two four sided stitch squares at each point of diamond

First part of Scand. edging stitch worked 6 threads beyond 'point' of diamond

FROM MY HANDS

Louisa's Opal
finished size 18 cm (7 in) square

I am constantly looking through old books and magazines for inspiration in my embroidery. There is a rich heritage of needlework to draw upon and I am fortunate to have acquired, over the years, an extensive library with a diverse selection of past embroideries and techniques. This design is adapted from a Sampler originally worked in 1651 and now held in the Victoria & Albert Museum.

Rather than stitching the satin stitch in this design 'white on white' I used one thread of a very pale coloured silk, Opal by Waterlilies and one thread of 'nearly white' silk. Whilst the appearance is still of a 'white' embroidery the faint hint of colour in Opal makes the satin stitch embroidery stand out much more.

Stitches used: counted satin stitch, eyelets, straight and four sided stitch, Holbein and Scandanavian edging stitch

In this pattern the Scandanavian edging stitch and four sided stitch are worked over three threads

It is recommended that you stitch this in the sequence given

Materials

- Louisa's Opal was stitched on a 25 cm square of Antique White Edinborough linen with 35 threads to the inch. Other linens could be used equally satisfactorily and the threads to use with the different linens are given in the table.
- 'Fine thread*' this is used as a general term and a variety of different threads are given which can be used. This design uses slightly heavier thread for the four sided stitch and second part of Scandanavian edging stitch.
- Matching stranded cotton or silk (one thread) and one thread of Opal, Waterlilies by Caron is used for the satin stitch flower shape. Use one thread for the eyelets.
- One thread of Coton a broder 25, satin stitch in the trellis shapes for linen with a thread count 28 – 36 for linen 19 – 25 use Coton a broder 16
- Matching Perle 12 for the first stage of Scandanavian edging stitch.
- Light coloured sewing cotton for tacking
- Tapestry needles Size 24 or 26
- Sharp needle - this can be useful for finishing off neatly

LOUISA'S OPAL

Important – Mark the top of the mat with coloured thread before you start working the fillings in the trellis framework. This thread will be removed later.

Louisa's Opal

linen - antique white	'fine thread*'	matching stranded cotton or silk,	
quantity required - numbers in bold equal threads per inch	threads used for four sided stitch, eyelets, 2nd part of Scandinavian edging stitch	threads used for counted satin stitch, Holbein stitch	threads used for 1st part of Scandinavian edging stitch
35 - 25 cm sq **(10 in sq)** **28 - 32** 30 cm sq (12 in sq)	• DMC Perle 12 • *DMC Coton a broder 25* • Londonderry linen thread 80/3 • Av Perlee • DMC Dentelles 80 for fabric with 19 – 30 threads per inch	two threads for flower shape *WC Opal* *AvD 3041 or Mode* D 819 M 1910 Kr 3011 A 271 • used in trellis shapes D Coton a broder 25	*D Perle 12* Av Perlee L 80/3 D Coton a broder 25
25 - 35 cm sq (14 in sq) **19 -** 40 cm sq (16 in sq)	• DMC Perle 8 • Coton a broder 16 • Londonderry linen thread 50/3 • Av Perlee • DMC Cordonnet 50	use three threads for satin stitch flower Coton a broder 16 for inside trellis shapes	D Perle 5 or 8 L 50/3 Kr Serica D Cordonnet 50

D = DMC **AvD** = Au Ver a Soie D'Alger **Kr** = Kreinik Mori **M** = Madeira **L** = Londonderry **WC** = Waterlilies by Caron

• The availability of threads varies around the world. We give alternatives which we know will give equal satisfaction in their use and create an equally beautiful design for you.

• Materials used shown in italics.

FROM MY HANDS

CHART A Top half of design
each line represents one thread

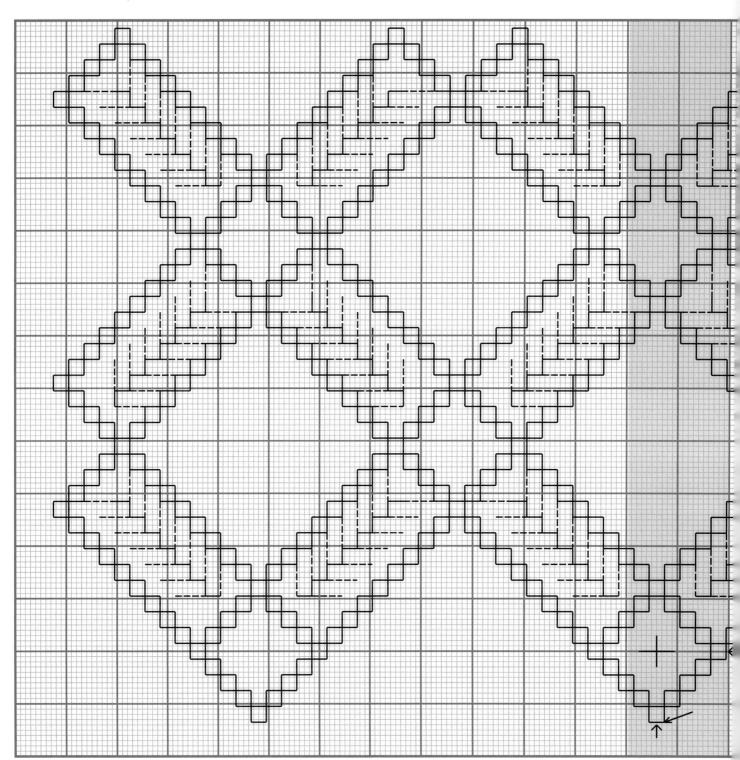

+ Centre of design
⌐ Holbein stitch
--- straight stitches
☐ four sided stitch
pattern overlap shaded

LOUISA'S OPAL

Instructions

Neaten the raw edge of your fabric first.
Fold the fabric in quarters to find the centre then tack accurately over and under three threads in both directions to mark the centre.
For more information on tacking see page 6.
All the four sided stitch is worked first.

Four sided stitch 'trellis' outlines

Chart A (the top half of the design)

In this design I wanted the trellis to have slightly more emphasis and for this reason I have used a heavier thread for the four sided stitching. Start at the central four sided stitch square (lower centre of chart A) using the long thread method (see page 11). Count down the tacking thread and work the four sided stitch square at the base of the diamond. See the arrow identifying the starting position.

Work all the four sided stitch to form the 'trellis frame' for the top half of the design. It is worked over three threads. Stitch using 'fine thread' and work each stitch only once. On completion of the trellis frame at the top of the design, continue with the trellis frame in the lower half of the design Chart B. See page 18 for more information on working four sided stitch on the diagonal.

Work on small sections at a time and keep checking that the four sided stitch squares line up with each other. Stitch the trellis carefully and your patience will be rewarded!

Pattern inside the rectangular *'trellis' frame*

Chart A - top half of design
Chart B - lower half of design

If you have not already marked the 'top' of your mat with a couple of stitches in coloured thread, do so now! The pattern inside the rectangles changes position and if you have not marked the top it is easy to become confused!

Using matching Coton a broder 25 work the zig zag found in each trellis rectangle in Holbein stitch. Carefully check the positioning of the zig zag line. *This stitching is important in establishing the position of the other stitching within this area.*

If you look at the photograph page 53 or charts A & B you will note that the embroidery within the trellis rectangle is next to the four sided stitch on every side of one square, but three threads away on

LOUISA'S OPAL

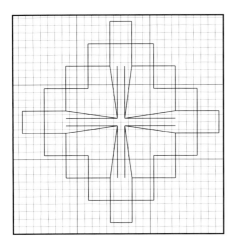

CHART C
each line represents one thread

Note at centre two threads into same space but each thread from a different position at outer edge

every side of the adjacent square. By following the positioning for the zig zag lines given this will happen automatically.

The straight stitches are actually *three* straight stitches worked in the same position using one thread of Coton a broder 25.
Stitch the pattern inside the trellis frames for the top half of the design. To complete the lower half of the design, refer to Chart B.

Eyelet *with Central Cross*

Refer to Chart C

Using Coton a broder 25 start at the outer edge of the eyelet, at the corner of the four sided stitch. Each stitch covers seven threads with two stitches into the same space at the centre but each thread comes from a different position at the outer edge. For information on starting and finishing threads see page 10.

Satin Stitch Pattern

Refer to Chart D

Thread your needle with one thread of 'nearly white' silk and one thread of Opal by Waterlilies. This design is positioned in the centre of each of the large diamonds created by the trellis framework. Normally I would start in the centre and work out but in this instance it is easier to position the satin stitch motif correctly if you count in 11 threads from the four sided stitch square at the 'point' of the diamond (see Chart D). On each side of the centre thread work the Holbein stitch 'curl'. Now work the satin stitch into the centre. Work from the centre out for the remaining sections, taking your thread back to the centre at the back of your work under the stitching, on the completion of each section.

Note each Holbein stitch is worked over two threads.

FROM MY HANDS

CHART B Lower half of design
each line represents one thread

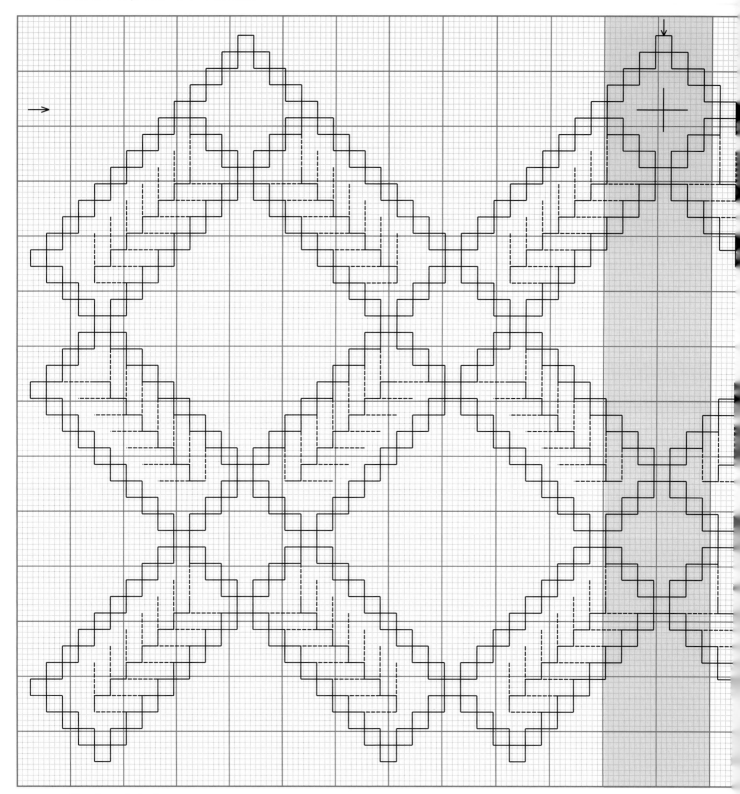

+ Centre of design
⌐ Holbein stitch
... straight stitches
☐ four sided stitch
pattern overlap shaded

LOUISA'S OPAL

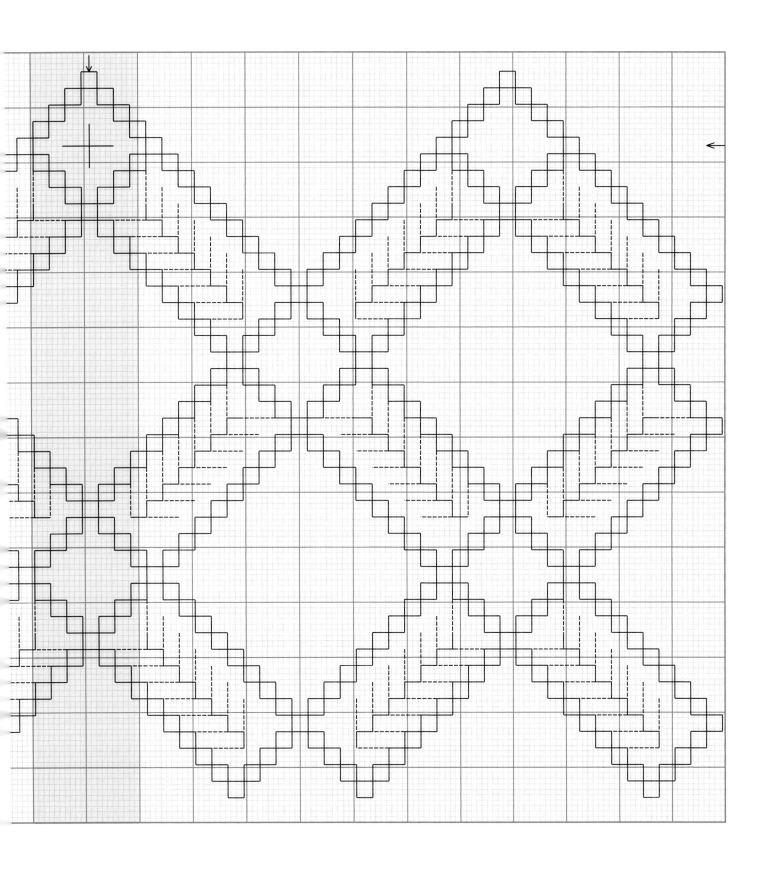

FROM MY HANDS

Eyelets

Chart D

These are stitched using one thread of silk and worked over two threads. Don't forget to use the stiletto! Start and finish thread for each eyelet in the eyelet. (For more information on circular eyelets see page 14)

Scandanavian *Edging Stitch*

(For detailed instructions on worked this stitch see page 18.)

Start near a corner. You will notice that the very outer square of four sided stitch on the trellis outline is directly above the edging. Count three threads out from the trellis rectangle and using matching Perle 12 work the first row of Scandanavian edging stitch, the stem stitch *on the wrong side* of your embroidery. Each stem stitch is worked going forward over six threads and back three threads.

When the hem is turned back at the stem stitch the second row of stitching is worked over three threads, making it just touch the trellis outline.

Work the final row of stitching using the fine thread used for the four sided stitch.

Louisa's Opal is beautiful design and I was very pleased with the end result.

CHART D
each line represents one thread

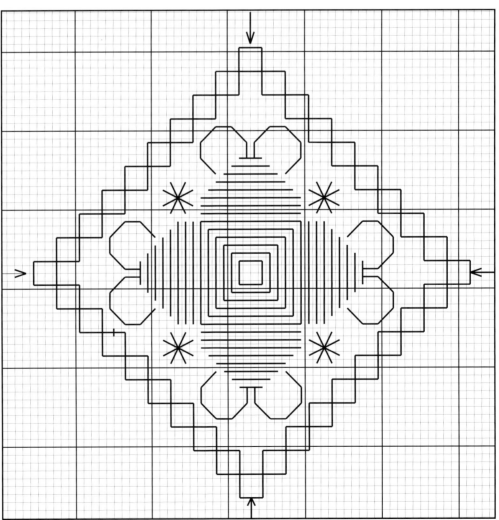

Bookmarks

Lavender Bags

Pink Simplicity

Danish Handkerchief

Danish Coasters

A tribute to Miss M.E. Roe

Needlework Accessories

Louisa's Opal

Blue Horizons

Paua Lights

A Danish Christmas

A Tribute to Miss M. E. Roe
finished size 21 cm (8 in) square

This is just one small square taken from the corner of a bedspread designed and stitched by a Miss M.E. Roe. I know very little of Miss Roe, her history, or other stitching accomplishments. I do know she taught embroidery for a 40 year period from the 1890's to the 1930's and lived at the Trent Rectory in Sherborne, England. The entire surface area of the bedspread was stitched. Miss Roe must have been very proud of this bedspread.

To achieve the richness and depth of colour found in 'A Tribute to Miss M. E. Roe' I stitched it on a deep cream Belfast linen, using deep cream thread. For a rich and more dramatic effect the stitching could be in light gold. Do experiment with these rich warm colours as the end result is very satisfying.

Stitches used: counted satin stitch, four sided stitch, eyelets, Scandanavian edging stitch

In this pattern the Scandanavian edging stitch and four sided stitch are worked over four threads

It is recommended that you stitch the design in the sequence given

Materials

- This mat was stitched on Belfast linen which has 31 threads to the inch. Alternative fabrics and the threads to use with them are given in the table.
- 'Fine thread'* this is used as a general term to apply to thread the weight and appearance of sewing cotton but either 100% cotton, silk or linen which is chosen to match the fabric. If a heavier thread is preferred DMC Perle 12 may be used in its place. (see notes under 'Five Central Four Sided Stitch Squares')
- Matching stranded cotton or silk for the satin stitch
- Tapestry needles Size 24 or 26
- Sharp needle - this can be useful for finishing off neatly
- 15 cm round embroidery frame

Instructions

Neaten the raw edge of your fabric first.
Fold the fabric in quarters to find the centre then tack over and under four threads in both directions to mark the centre. Refer to page 6 for more tacking information.

Five Central Four Sided Stitch Squares

Refer to Chart A
Do not pull the four sided stitches too tightly, satin stitch will be worked in this area next.

To begin, work the five four sided stitch squares in the centre of the design. Thread your needle with the 'fine thread'* or Perle 12. If you

A Tribute to Miss M. E. Roe

linen - deep cream	'fine thread'*	stranded cotton or silk	
quantity required numbers in bold equal threads per inch	threads used for four sided stitch, eyelets, 2nd part of Scandinavian edging stitch,	threads used for counted satin stitch	threads used for 1st part of Scandinavian edging stitch
36 20cm sq (8 in square) **31** 25cm sq (10 in square) **28** 25cm sq (10 in square)	• *Madeira Cotona* • Zwicky 100% cotton or silk Guterman 100 % silk or cotton • Au Ver a Soie 1003 100% silk • Londonderry Linen thread 80/3 • Dewhurst Sylko • DMC Dentelles 80 for fabric with 19 – 30 threads per inch	two threads D 677 AvD 2542 M 2014 A 886	*D Perle 12* Av Perlee Kr Serica L 30/3 *2 strands of silk thread used in satin stitch*
25 - 30 cm sq (9 in sq) **19** - 35 cm sq (14 in sq)	• DMC Cordonnet 80 • Coton a broder 25 • Perle 12 • Au Ver a Soie Perlee	use three threads for satin stitch on linen 19 – 25 threads to the inch	Perle 5 & 8 L 18/3

D = DMC **AvD** = Au Ver a Soie D'Alger **M** = Madeira **L** = Londonderry Linen Thread **A** = Anchor

• The availability of threads varies around the world. We give alternatives which we know will give equal satisfaction in their use and create an equally beautiful design for you.

• Materials used are shown in italics.

A TRIBUTE TO MISS M.E. ROE

use fine thread each stitch will need to be stitched twice. To do this, do not complete one four sided stitch and then work a second four sided stitch on top of the first. Rather stitch each part of the four sided stitch twice as you go. I do this because I like the clear, precise finish that is achieved when working with it this way. However if you use Perle 12 each stitch only needs to be worked once.

Count out 14 threads from the centre, your needle is now on the bottom line of the row of four sided stitch. Take your needle two threads to the right (see arrow indicating starting point on the chart). Work four squares in four sided stitch, this takes you to the corner. Turn the corner and complete the entire central square. For detailed information on working four sided stitch and turning corners, refer to page 17.

CHART A
each line represents
one thread

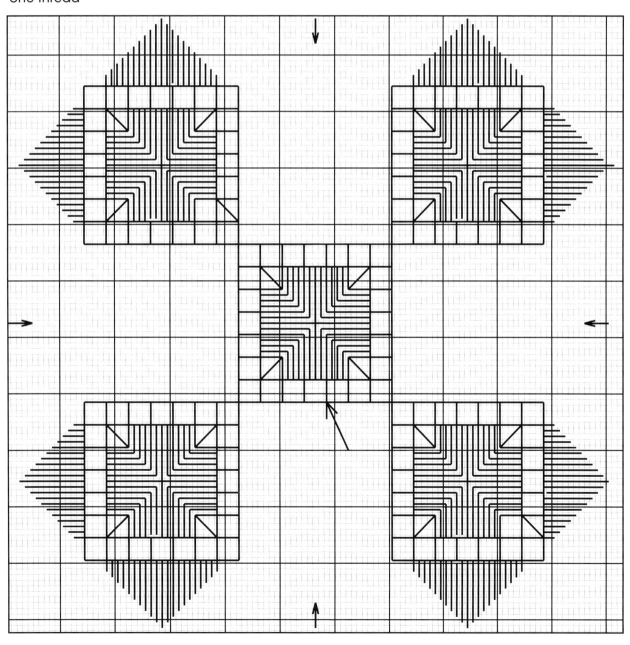

On completion of the central square take your thread through the stitches at the back of your work to a corner and work the next four sided stitch square. Complete all five of the four sided stitch squares.

Satin stitch is worked using two threads of stranded silk or cotton throughout.

Satin Stitch Centres *and* Triangles Outside Squares

Refer to Chart B, this shows an enlarged detail from Chart A

Thread your needle with two threads of stranded cotton or silk and bring your needle out four threads from the corner. Work satin stitch over four threads. Stitch from the corner into the centre covering an extra thread with each stitch. When working from the centre back out to the corner cover one less thread with each stitch. Stop four threads from the corner and work the diagonal stitch into the corner. Fill all four sides of the square and then repeat in each of the remaining four squares.

CHART B
each line represents one thread

On the outer squares there are two satin stitch triangles outside the four sided stitch square, work these on completion of the satin stitch inside each square. Note these triangles are stitched starting one four sided stitch in from the corner. Work following the chart.

Satin Stitch Carnation *extending from each corner*

Refer to Chart C

Next work the six satin stitch blocks (three stitches over six threads) out to the carnation. The first block of three stitches over six threads is worked over the last three threads up to the corner and three threads beyond the corner. Working from the chart complete the carnation.

Satin Stitch Star *extending from the central square*

Refer to Chart D

This motif is positioned at the centre of each side of the central four sided stitch square. The first satin stitch is worked over two threads,

A TRIBUTE TO MISS M.E. ROE

CHART C
each line represents one thread

tack 16 stitches under and over four from points shown for placement of inner square of four sided border

one thread out from the four sided stitch square. Work out to the star. To work the satin stitch star, begin at the centre of the star working one section of the star at a time. The first stitch is over two threads and in the following rows one side of the star is kept straight, whilst the other side is worked over an extra thread in each row. At the ninth row this is reversed, the side that was straight now decreases one thread per line and the other side has a straight edge. When you have completed one section of the star take your needle under the stitching at the back of your work to the centre ready to begin the next section. Repeat each side of the centre square.

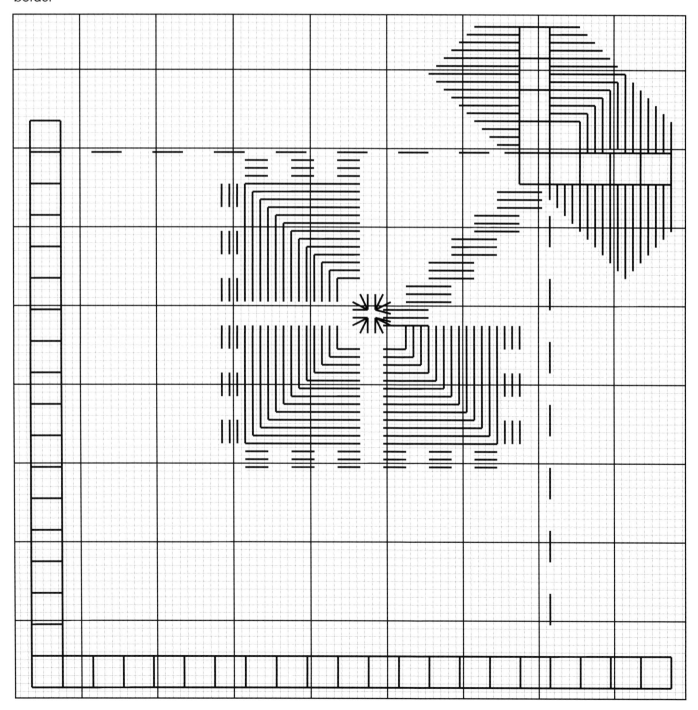

Eyelets

The eyelets are all worked with 'fine thread' or one thread of stranded cotton or silk. Refer to page 13 for detailed instructions on working the different eyelets. Remember to use a stiletto to achieve a nicely shaped circle.

Small Circular Eyelet *at Centre of Star*

Refer to Chart D

This is just a 'suggestion' of an eyelet. It is worked with fine cotton over two threads.

Star Tip Eyelets

Refer to Chart D

The circular eyelets at the tip of each section of the star are worked over three threads.

Single Cross *Eyelet*

Refer to Chart C

The eyelet at the centre of the Carnation is a single cross eyelet. This eyelet has been worked right up to the satin stitches and there is not sufficient space to continue working the eyelet exactly as shown in the stitch section, so work following the chart and when you reach the satin stitch, work the stitches between the satin stitches to pull the thread back.

CHART D
••• indicates where each stitch ends

each line represents one thread

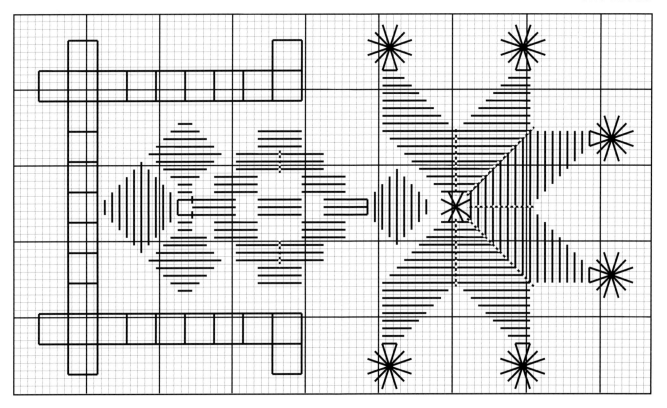

Border

Refer to Chart C

To position the four sided stitch border correctly, run a tacking thread under and over four threads in both directions from the outer edges of each of the four sided stitch outer squares - see Chart C. Count down 16 of the tacking stitches and start working four sided stitch from this point. This is the lower edge of your line of four sided stitch. Work from the tacked line to the corners, to ensure the lines of stitching meet! Stitch using a fine thread and working each stitch twice or use Perle 12 and work each stitch once.

Refer to Chart E

Now work the satin stitch border using two threads of stranded cotton or silk. This block of three stitches is worked over six threads. It is best to start the border design going into a corner, see arrow Chart E. At the corner these stitches are 'mitred' - refer to the chart. The two triangles in the corner are worked last.

Work the outer four sided stitch border. Note the satin stitch border is only one thread from the four sided stitch inner border but four threads from the outer four sided stitch border.

Scandanavian *Four Sided* Edging Stitch

for detailed instructions on worked this stitch see page 18

CHART E
Arrow shows position to start satin stitch

each line represents one thread

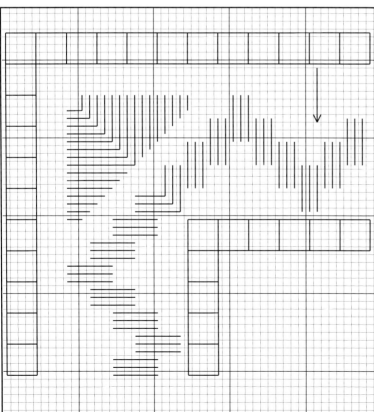

Using matching Perle 12 work the first row of Scandanavian edging stitch, the stem stitch, going forward over eight threads and back four threads each time. It is worked on the wrong side of the fabric. Start near the corner lining it up directly beneath the four sided stitch border. Work the final row of Scandanavian edging stitching using the 'fine thread' or Perle 12 used for the four sided stitch.

I found a picture of Miss Roe's bedspread in a 1916 Embroideress magazine. The influence of Louisa Pesel, a leading English embroiderer at the turn of the century and authoress of 'Historical Designs for Embroidery', can be seen in this design.

FROM MY HANDS

Needlework Accessories

needle book finished size 9 cm (3 in) square

pin cushion 9 cm (3 in) square

scissors fob 5.5 cm (2 in) square

Needlework Accessories are a necessity for the embroiderer and a treasured gift for a friend. They are also a great way to try out a new technique or design. This set does not require a big time commitment but will give much satisfaction in its creation. Counted satin stitch always looks most attractive and contrasts well with the texture of four sided stitch. We have stitched this on Crushed Strawberry with toning shades for the embroidery. You could of course stitch it on any coloured linen and stitch it in colours to match your work basket!

Stitches used: counted satin, eyelet, four sided stitch, nun's stitch, Scandanavian edging stitch and chain edging

In this pattern the Scandanavian edging, nun's and four sided stitches are worked over three threads

It is recommended that you stitch the design in the sequence given

Materials

- This set was stitched on Legacy, Crushed Strawberry linen with 30 threads to the inch. All embroidery is toning. Alternative fabrics and the threads to use with them are given in the table.
- 'Fine thread*' this is used as a general term to apply to thread the weight and appearance of sewing cotton but either 100% cotton, silk or linen which is chosen to match the fabric, see table. This is used for the four sided stitch, eyelets and Scandanavian edging.
- Matching stranded cotton or silk for the satin stitch and chain stitch edging
- Tapestry needles Size 24 or 26
- Sharp needle - this can be useful for finishing off neatly
- Tacking thread
- 15 cm embroidery hoop

Instructions

Neaten the raw edge of your fabric. The three items are all made out of the one piece of linen.
Fold the linen into thirds, see Fig. 1 Then tack a line lengthways down the centre of each third. The needlebook is worked in the top third, the Pincushion in the centre and the scissors fob at the base.

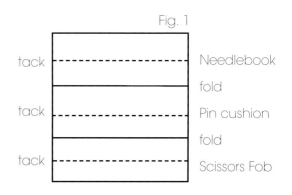

Fig. 1

NEEDLEWORK ACCESSORIES

Needlebook

The needlebook uses the satin stitch design from Paua Lights. This design could be featured front and back or you could put your initials and the date on the reverse.

Needlework Accessories

linen crushed strawberry	'fine thread*'	matching stranded cotton or silk
quantity required numbers in bold equal threads per inch	threads used for four sided stitch, eyelets, 2nd part of Scandinavian edging stitch	threads used for counted satin stitch and 1st and 2nd part of Scandinavian edging stitch
35 25 x 35 cm (10 x 14 in) **30** *30 x 45 cm (12 x 18 in)* **28** 30 x 45 cm (12 x 18 in)	• Zwicky 100% cotton or silk • *Guterman 100 % silk or cotton* • Au Ver a Soie 1003 100% silk • Madeira Cotona • Dewhurst Sylko • DMC Dentelles 80 for use in linen 19 – 30 threads to the inch	**D** 352 ***AvD** 932* **M** 0303 **A** 9
25 30 x 45 cm (12 x 18 in) **19** 35 x 50 cm (14 x 20 in)	• Coton a broder 25 • DMC Perle 12 • Cordonnet 80 • Londonderry linen thread 80/3	Use three threads for satin stitch on 19 – 25 linen

D = DMC **Av** = Au Ver a Soie D'Alger **M** = Madeira **A** = Anchor

- The availability of threads varies around the world. We give alternatives which we know will give equal satisfaction in their use and create an equally beautiful design for you.
- Materials used shown in italics.

Four Sided Stitch *Centre*

With the tacked line in the top third of your fabric as a guide measure in 2 cms (1 in) from the side and start working four sided stitch at the side 'point' of the diamond, using matching coloured fine thread. There are 17 four sided stitch squares worked over three threads down the diagonal of each side of the outer diamond. Note there are two four sided stitches in line at the 'point'. Refer to page 18 for more information on stitching four sided stitch on the diagonal.

On completion of the outer square run the thread through your stitches at the back of the work to the correct position to work the first diagonal line in to the smaller square. Stitch this then work the inner square, stitching the connecting lines as you come to them bringing the thread back to the inner square through the stitching at the back of your work.

Satin Stitch Designs

These are worked using two threads of matching stranded cotton or silk. Stitch the satin stitch design in the centre of the square and then work the four motifs found outside the square. Start stitching the motif at the centre, stitch one side then turn your work around and stitch back along the other side. Note the dotted line through the centre of the design indicates where each stitch finishes.

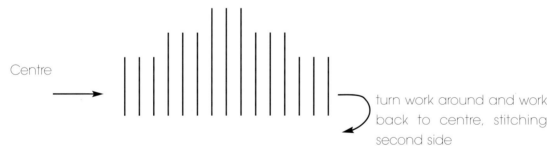

Eyelets

Work the square eyelet found in the centre of the satin stitch design with the fine thread used for working the four sided stitch. Refer to page 13 for more information on stitching eyelets.

Scandanavian *Edging Stitch*

Follow the chart, the dashed outer line shows where the first row of Scandanavian edging stitch, the stem stitch, is worked using two threads of stranded cotton or silk. It is stitched *on the wrong side* of the fabric three threads beyond the 'points' of the outer four sided stitch diamond. Stitch right round the outside edge of the needlebook, front and back cover and down the centre for the spine

NEEDLEWORK ACCESSORIES

CHART A
every line represents one thread

• • • indicates end of stitch

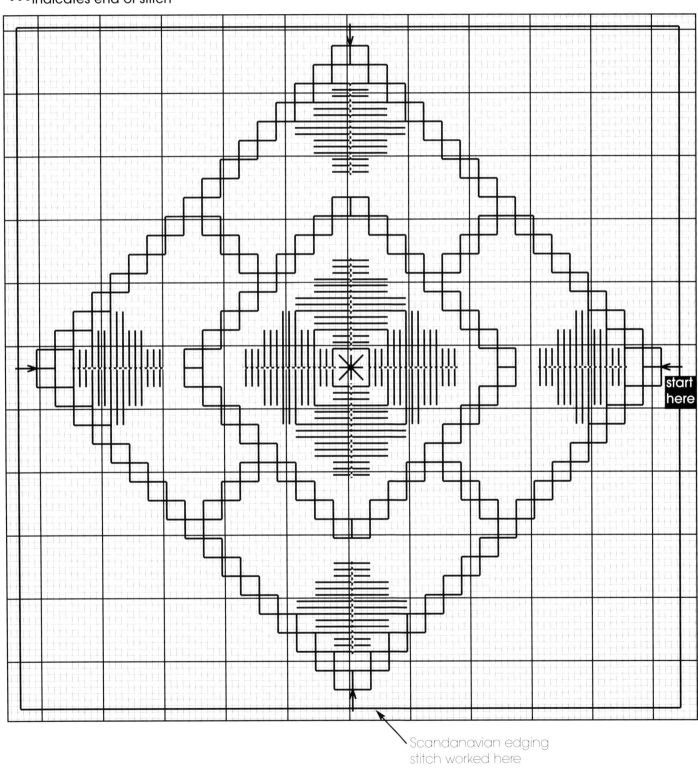

Scandanavian edging stitch worked here

67

(see chart). Each stitch is worked going forward over six threads and back over three. Start directly beneath one of the 'points' using the long thread method. This will enable you to position the Scandanavian edging stitch directly beneath the four sided stitch accurately. See page 11 for more information on starting using the long thread method.

The second row of Scandanavian edging stitch is worked with the thread used for the four sided stitch. It is worked right round the perimeter of the needle book but NOT down the spine.

there are 36 Scandanavian edging stitches up to the centre (spine). Do not work second part of Scand. edging stitch along the spine

36

36 36

The design on the back cover is started six threads from the side 'point' of the front cover

To Make Up

Cut a piece of matching coloured silk to fit inside the needlebook and turn the raw edges under before slip stitching it to the inside of the Scandanavian edging stitch. Cut two pieces of Doctor's flannel for the needlebook pages to fit inside the needlebook. I cut the inside page smaller than the outside one so that the edges are not 'bulky'. Neaten the edges by working nun's stitch, buttonhole or machine sew.

Attach the pages down the centre spine invisibly, either do a back stitch or running stitch and then work a row of chain stitch on top of the back stitch to finish.

PINCUSHION
each line represents one thread

solid outline reverse chain stitch to be worked here

•••dotted line indicates where each stitch ends

NEEDLEWORK ACCESSORIES

Pincushion

This is a repeat of the motif used on the front of the needlebook. Stitch following the instructions given in the Needle Book starting at the 'Four Sided Stitch Centre' and continue up to and including the 'Eyelet'. Repeat for the back of the pincushion - once again you may like to include your initials and date in the centre rather than the satin stitch design

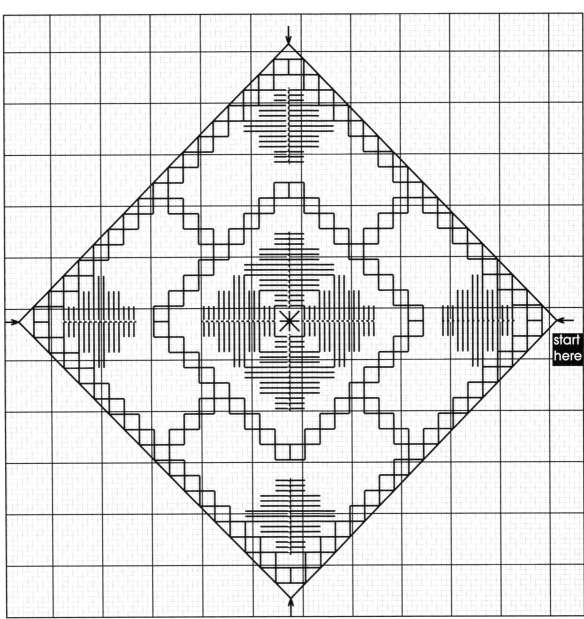

Edging

This pincushion has a different edging - it is joined by reverse chain stitch. I work reverse chain stitch as I find it gives a better tension and is easier to stitch accurately on counted thread than ordinary chain stitch, see page 20 for detailed instructions on working reverse chain stitch.

Using two threads of stranded cotton work reverse chain stitch from point to point (see solid line on chart) along the outside edge of the four sided stitch. Note that the chain stitch is worked to form a point. Do this on both sides of the pincushion. Cut off excess fabric but leave 10 mm to fold in. Then hold the two sides of the pincushion together, matching stitches and whip the two chain stitched edges together on three sides. This makes a very dainty edging.

To Complete

Make a separate matching silk lining for the pincushion, stuff then place inside the pincushion. Finish sewing the pincushion together.

Make four tassels 5.5 cm in length with the threads from the satin stitching and attach at the centre of each side of the pincushion.

SCISSOR'S FOB
each line represents one thread

solid outline reverse chain stitch to be worked here

•••dotted line indicates where each stitch ends

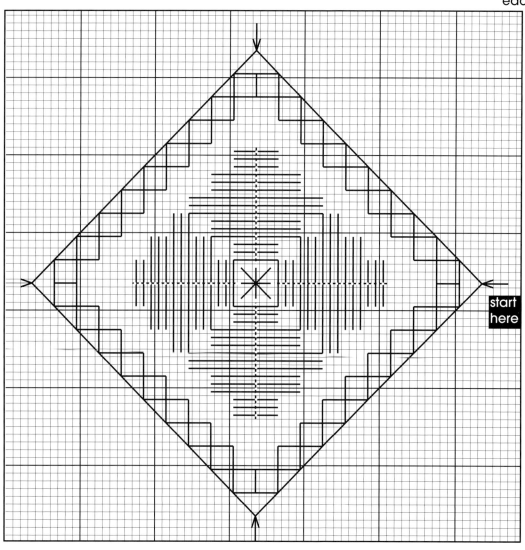

start here

Scissors fob

With the tacked line in the bottom third of your fabric as a guide measure in 2 cms (1 in) from the side and start working four sided stitch at the side 'point' of the diamond, using matching coloured fine thread. There are 9 four sided stitch squares worked over three threads down the diagonal of each side of the diamond. Refer to page 18 for more information on stitching four sided stitch on the diagonal.

Next work the central satin stitch design and eyelet following the instructions given with the Needle Book. Then work reverse chain from point to point (see solid line on chart) along the outside of the four sided stitch. Note to work reverse chain to form a point. Repeat for the reverse side of the fob.

Then hold the two sides of the scissors fob together, matching stitches and whip the two chain stitched edges on three sides. Make a completely separate matching silk lining for the scissors fob. Then cut two pieces of felt slightly smaller than the finished square to fit inside the lining and place felt and lining inside the embroidered fob. Whip the final side together. To complete, attach a little cord at one tip and join the scissors to this.

Your needlework set is complete. This needlework set could be made by taking motifs out of a number of the designs and changing the size of the four sided stitch square surrounding the motif to create a quite different look. Do enjoy experimenting and stitching!

FROM MY HANDS

A Danish *Christmas*
finished size 15 x 45 cm (6 x 18 in)

Christmas. We celebrate Christmas in many different ways. For those of us in the Southern Hemisphere it is a time of sunshine, summer holidays, barbecues, beaches and swimming. For those in the Northern Hemisphere Christmas is celebrated midwinter with cold temperatures and hot food. This Christmas design is an adaptation of an eighteenth century Danish nursery design featuring motifs that we can all relate to, Christmas trees, reindeer and hearts. This distinctive design, with its splendid tassels and luxuriant fringing, is a decoration worthy of pride of place in your home in either hemisphere.

Stitches used: Eyelet, double cross, straight, counted satin, four sided stitch and Scandanavian edging stitch

In this pattern four sided stitch and Scandanavian edging stitch are worked over four threads

It is recommended that you stitch the design in the sequence given

Materials

- This has been stitched on Legacy Parchment linen with 30 threads to the inch. I chose a natural coloured linen as I felt that was closer to the type of linen that would have been used in the eighteenth century. I chose DMC Perle 12 threads to work with as I like their sheen, but a truly authentic appearance would be achieved by using linen threads. This design could be stitched on linen with a different thread count per inch and would look equally attractive. Alternative fabrics and the threads to use with them are given in the table.
- DMC Light Gold Thread DM 282
- Tapestry Needle 24 or 26
- Tacking thread
- 15 cm embroidery hoop

Instructions

The photograph shows the entire design which has three pattern repeats or nine rows of pattern in total. Chart A gives the first three rows of the pattern plus part of the fourth row. It also gives the top and side borders to show how the motifs are placed in relation to each other and the borders. *The positioning of the heart in the top row is different from its placement in all other rows.* Chart B shows the

A DANISH CHRISTMAS

last row of pattern with the border design. It also shows the placement of the Scandanavian edging stitch on each side and the four sided stitch at the base.

Neaten the raw edges of the fabric. Fold in half lengthwise and run a tacking thread up the centre stitching over and under four threads. Measure down 5 cm from the top of the fabric at the centre and you are ready to begin stitching the reindeer.

Full instructions for working individual eyelet stitches are given on page 13. However it is easier to work rows of eyelet stitches a little

A Danish Christmas

linen - natural coloured

quantity required - numbers in bold equal threads per inch	threads for eyelets, double cross stitches, four sided stitch and Scandinavian edging stitch	threads for counted satin stitch - stranded cotton or silk
35 20 x 50 cm (8 x 20 in) *30 Legacy Parchment Linen* 20 x 50 cm (8 x 20 in) **28** 20 x 60 cm (8 x 24 in)	• *DMC Perle 12, 699, 666, 640* • Au Ver a Soie Perlee 620, 664, 516 • Kreinik Serica 4037, 1116, 7024 • Londonderry Linen Thread 30/3 • Wild Rose, Evergreen, Clove Brown	Two threads **D** *699, 666, 640* **AvD** 945, 146, 3345 **M** 1303, 0210, 1905 **Kr** 4037, 1116, 7024 **A** 923, 9046, 903
25 20 x 60 cm (8 x 24 in) **19** 30 x 60 cm (12 x 24 in)	• Perle 8 • Coton a broder 16 • Three threads of stranded cotton	Use three threads of above colours for satin stitch using 19 & 25 count linen

D = DMC **AvD** = Au Ver a Soie D'Alger **AvP** = Perlee **M** = Madeira **A** = Anchor

- The availability of threads varies around the world. We give alternatives which we know will give equal satisfaction in their use and create an equally beautiful design for you.
- Material used shown in italics.

FROM MY HANDS

differently. See instructions under 'To Stitch the Reindeer' and 'To Stitch the Tree'.

It is important to remember that you always take your needle down in the centre of each eyelet.

To stitch the Reindeer
(Chart A)

This is stitched using DMC Perle 12 Taupe thread throughout. Referring to Chart A and fig. 1 bring your needle out in the correct position to work the first row of three eyelet stitches to form the top antler. Note the position of the first stitch. Always work from right to left, turning your work as required. Work the top half of the first eyelet then referring to fig. 1 bring the needle out in the correct position (X) to work the top half of the second eyelet and then the top half of the third eyelet which completes the row. Now finish the third eyelet and work back across the row completing each eyelet (fig. 2).

If at any stage in your embroidery you find you cannot move across to the correct position for the next eyelet in this manner, just run your thread through the stitching at the back of the work until you are in the right spot!

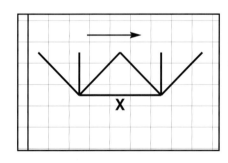

Fig. 1
Come back out at X and start to work the next eyelet

Always take your needle down in the centre of each eyelet

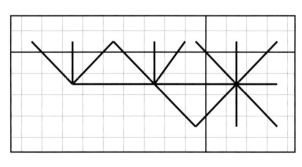

Fig. 2
Finish third eyelet and work back across the row completing each eyelet.

To Stitch the *Tree*
(Chart A)

This is worked using green DMC Perle 12 for the tree, red for the double cross stitches and light metallic gold for the candles. Run a

A DANISH CHRISTMAS

CHART A
each line represents one thread

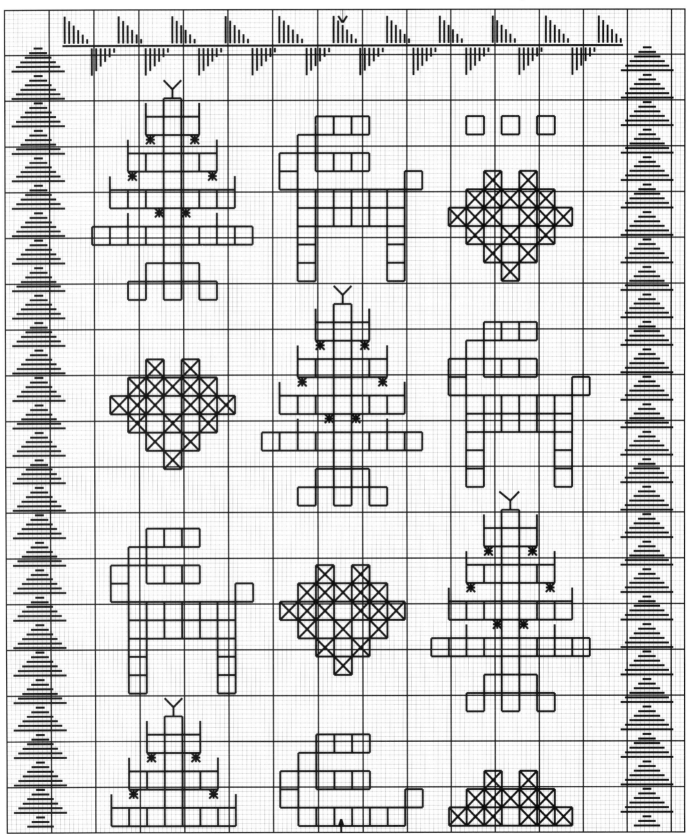

tacking thread from the reindeer across to the tree to find the correct starting position.

Start with the single eyelet at the top and work down. The top half of the centre eyelet in the next row is worked as shown in fig. 3 then stitching is continued as for the row described in the 'reindeer'. The left hand eyelet is stitched at the end of the row, see fig. 4. To stitch the single eyelet below this row, bring the needle out at A. Continue stitching in this manner to complete the tree.

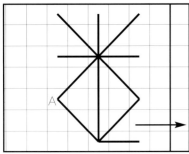

Fig. 3
Bring your needle out at A to work the first stitch in the next eyelet, your needle will go down at the centre of the eyelet.

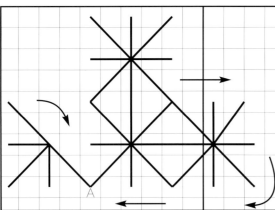

Fig. 4
Work in the direction of the arrows, working the top of each eyelet along the row as shown in fig.2. Then work back completing each eyelet. The left hand eyelet is stitched at the end of the row. To stitch the single eyelet below this row, bring the needle out at A.

The double cross stitches are worked in red and the candles are straight stitches worked in gold over three threads, (stitched twice). These embellishments are not added until all the trees have been completed .

Handy Hint If you find metallic threads hard to use - separate the strands of metallic thread and use one strand of metallic thread together with one thread of a yellow stranded cotton and you will find the metallic thread much easier to use!

To Stitch the *Heart*

(Chart A)
Tack across from the reindeer to find the correct starting position for the heart. It is stitched using the techniques described in the 'Tree' and 'Reindeer' and using DMC Perle 12 red throughout.

Handy Hint This Christmas Design could be made any shape by adding or subtracting motifs.

To Continue the Pattern

After you have worked the first row of the pattern, for the remaining eight rows it is easier to ensure the correct placement of your motifs if you work the tree first in each row, counting down from the reindeer's front foot. On completion of the tree, stitch the reindeer and heart. Count from the centre row of the tree (third branch down) to the top line of eyelets which form the reindeer's body and then work up and down from there. Similarly count across from the third branch of the tree to the third to top line of the heart. The stitching techniques described above work extremely well and make this quite quick to stitch. Stitch all nine rows of the pattern before stitching the borders.

To Stitch the Side Borders

(Chart A)

Using two threads of stranded cotton, follow the chart and work the counted satin stitch border. It is easiest to work this by threading two needles, one with red and the other green then stitch the border, changing needles as required. Leave the needle not in use on top of your fabric so that you do not tangle threads. Slip the thread through the stitching at the back of your work on the way down, ready to bring the needle out in the correct starting position for the next triangle.

To Stitch the Top and Bottom Borders

(Charts A and B)

Following the chart and using two threads of taupe stranded cotton, stitch the satin stitch border design. Using two threads of green stranded cotton work stem stitch along the centre of the border. The stem stitch is worked going forward four threads and back two.

To Finish the Sides

Chart B

Using the green thread you used for the trees, work the first part of Scandanavian edging stitch, the stem stitch, *on the wrong side* of the fabric. It is worked down each side of the design. Start near the top and count eight threads out from the counted satin stitch border. Work up to the top edge of the fabric and down to just below the lower border pattern at the base of the design. Go up eight threads and back four for each stem stitch (see page 18 for detailed information on Scandanavian edging stitch). To ensure that the edging stitches line up, run a tacking thread across the top from the first side to the starting position of the second side.

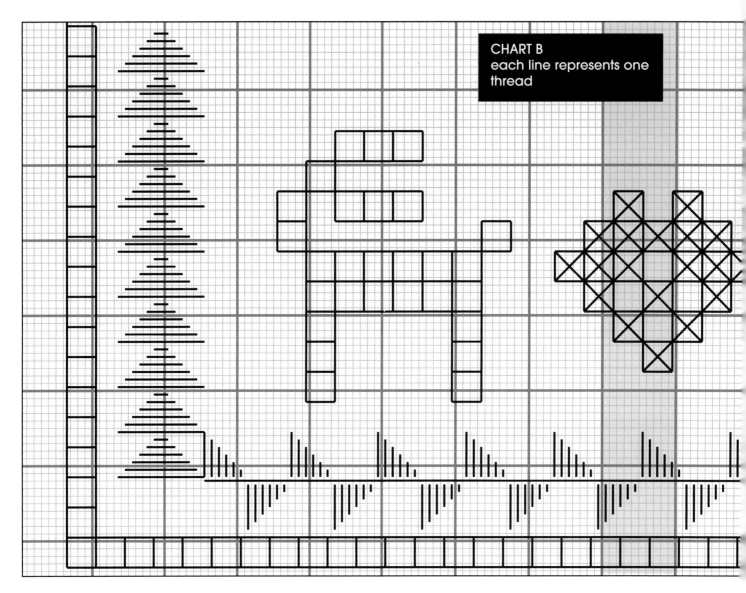

CHART B
each line represents one thread

The second part of Scandanavian edging stitch is worked using the taupe thread the reindeer were stitched with.

To finish the Base

Work four sided stitch across the base of the hanging, between the Scandanavian edging stitch on each side, using the taupe thread from the reindeer, (see Chart B). Then pull the threads out beyond the four sided stitch to make a fringe.

To create a more luxuriant fringe I added extra threads. To do this cut a length of taupe thread a little longer than the desired length of the fringe. Thread the two ends through the eye of the needle. Take your needle up under the bottom stitch in your four sided stitch edging and pick up a small amount of fabric (fig. 5) then take your needle back through the thread loop and pull down firmly (fig. 6). Position the knot at the base of the hanging. Do this into each stitch all the way across the bottom of the hanging.

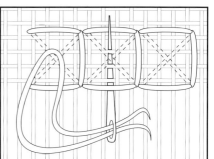

Fig 5.

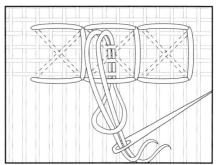

Fig 6.

A DANISH CHRISTMAS

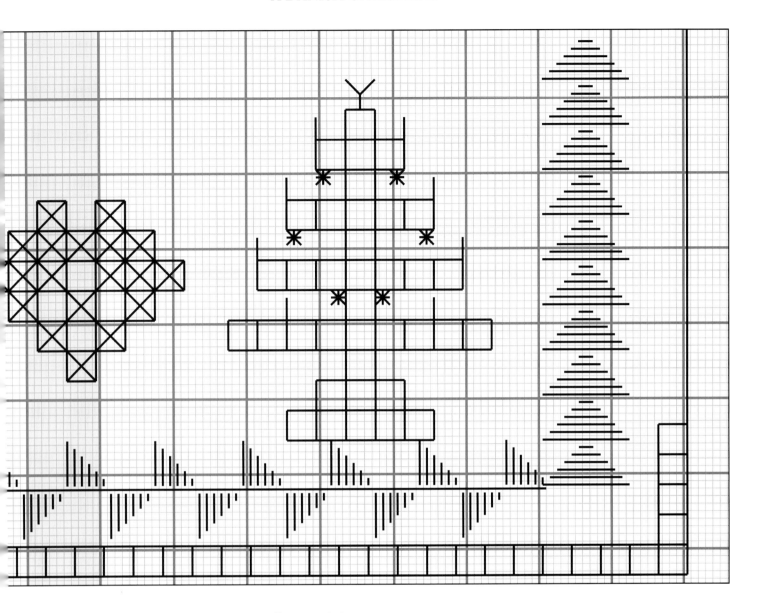

Handy Hint
If any adjustments need to be made when stitching four sided stitch, work two stitches over three threads rather than one over six

To complete

Turn the hem down at the top leaving sufficient space for the brass Bell Pull to fit nicely. Fold under the raw edge and hem stitch in place using matching thread.

I have used a brass Bell Pull hanger, but a wooden or bamboo skewer would also work well, with a plaited length of the red, green and taupe threads to make a hanging cord.

Use the red and green embroidery cottons to make two tassels 15 cm in length. Cover the head of the tassel with detached buttonhole stitch and attach so that the base of the head of the tassel is resting at the bottom edge of the hanging.

Each Christmas hang this up with pride for your family and friends to enjoy.

Paua *Lights*

finished size 32 cm (12 in) square

Paua Lights was inspired by the very pretty colours found in the New Zealand paua shell. Frequently seen along the seashore, the paua has a rather dull exterior but a multi coloured interior. The interior can be quite strongly coloured or quite subtle. I decided to play with the subtle shades and used four different, softly coloured silks to stitch the satin stitch design. In some lights the variations are barely noticeable, in others the colours look very different indeed. Stitch Paua Lights in the colours given or buy linen and threads in tones you prefer. This design could be enlarged right up to tablecloth size by extending the distance between the squares.

This design is also used in a needlework accessory set. Sometimes you want to stitch on a small scale. This set gives you the opportunity to try out the pattern while making something every stitcher needs! See page 64 for instructions to make the Needlework Accessory Set.

Stitches used: counted satin, eyelet, four sided stitch and Scandanavian edging stitch

In this pattern the Scandanavian edging and four sided stitch are worked over three threads

It is recommended that you stitch the design in the sequence given

Materials

- This mat was stitched on a 40cm square of gray Edinborough linen with 35 threads to the inch. Other linens could also be used with equal satisfaction and the threads to use with the different linens are given in the table.
- 'Fine thread*' this is used as a general term to apply to thread with the weight and appearance of sewing cotton but either 100% cotton, silk or linen which is chosen to match the fabric.
- Stranded cotton or silk for the satin stitch. I used four different threads for the satin stitch using one thread of gray (with one thread of three other soft toning colours to create the subtle colour variations -Waterlilies Crystal Bay, Blush and Ice
- Tapestry needles Size 24 or 26
- Sharp needle - this can be useful for finishing off neatly
- 15 cm Embroidery Hoop

PAUA LIGHTS

Instructions

Neaten the raw edge of your fabric first.

Fold the fabric in quarters to find the centre then tack over and under three threads in both directions to mark the centre. Refer to chart A for placement of additional tacking threads to ensure correct placement of the design. (See page 6 for additional information on tacking.)

Paua Lights

linen - gray	'fine thread'*	stranded cotton or silk	
quantity required - numbers in bold equal threads per inch	threads for four sided stitch, eyelets, 2nd part of Scandinavian edging stitch	threads for counted satin stitch	threads for 1st part of Scandinavian edging stitch
Fabric used 35 threads to the inch **32 - 35** 40 cm sq. (15 in sq.) **30** 45 cm sq. (18 in sq.) **28** 50 cm sq. (20 in sq.)	• Zwicky 100% cotton or silk • Guterman 100 % silk or cotton • Au Ver a Soie 1003 100% silk • *Madeira Cotona* • Dewhurst Sylko • Londonderry linen thread 100/3 • DMC Dentelles 80 for fabric with 19 - 30 threads per inch	two threads of **WC** *Crystal Bay, Blush, Ice* **D** 747, 3770, 3753, 762 **Av** *1721, 1011, 1431, 3441* **M** 1104, 0306, 1001, 1804 **A** 158, 1009, 1031, 234	**D** Perle 12 **Av** Perlee **WC** *Two threads of stranded cotton or silk - Blush*
25 50 cm sq. (20 in sq.) **19** 80 cm sq. (30 in sq.)	• Coton a broder 16 • DMC Perle 16 • Londonderry linen thread 80/3	use three threads of the above colours on linen 19 - 25 threads per inch	**D** Perle 8 Three threads of stranded cotton or silk

D = DMC **Av** = Au Ver a Soie D'Alger **M** = Madeira **L** = Londonderry **A** = Anchor
WC = Waterlilies by Caron

• The availability of threads varies around the world. We give alternatives which we know will give equal satisfaction in their use and create an equally beautiful design for you.

• Materials used shown in italics.

FROM MY HANDS

All the four sided stitch is worked before stitching the satin stitch and eyelets. For additional information on stitching four sided stitch on the diagonal refer to page 18.

There are three charts given with Paua Lights. Chart A shows the *centre* with the four diagonal lines of four sided stitch coming out from the centre to the next squares stitched. Chart B shows *one quarter of the entire design*, Chart C shows an enlarged detail of the satin stitch motif.

Centre
(refer to Chart A)

The four sided stitch is worked using matching coloured fine thread, sew each stitch once. The lower edge of the four sided stitch is worked 27 threads (or nine of the tacked stitches) out from the centre.

Follow the chart and work four sided stitch to create the central square which contains the satin stitch design. Next work the four sided stitch diagonal lines coming out from the centre of each side of the square, leading to a further square. Work each square as you come to it. **All squares are the same size as the central square.** This is where the extra tacking lines come in handy to check that the squares are correctly positioned!

From this point on refer to Chart B. This shows one quarter of the entire design - the centre is now positioned at the bottom right hand corner of the chart and the area already worked is shaded. Work one quarter of the design at a time. Stitch all the diagonal four sided stitch lines out from your completed stitching towards the squares which are positioned on the sides of the design at the centre and in the corner and work each square as you come to it.

Finally work the four sided stitch lines and squares on the outer edge of Paua Lights linking up the existing squares.

CHART A
each line represents one thread

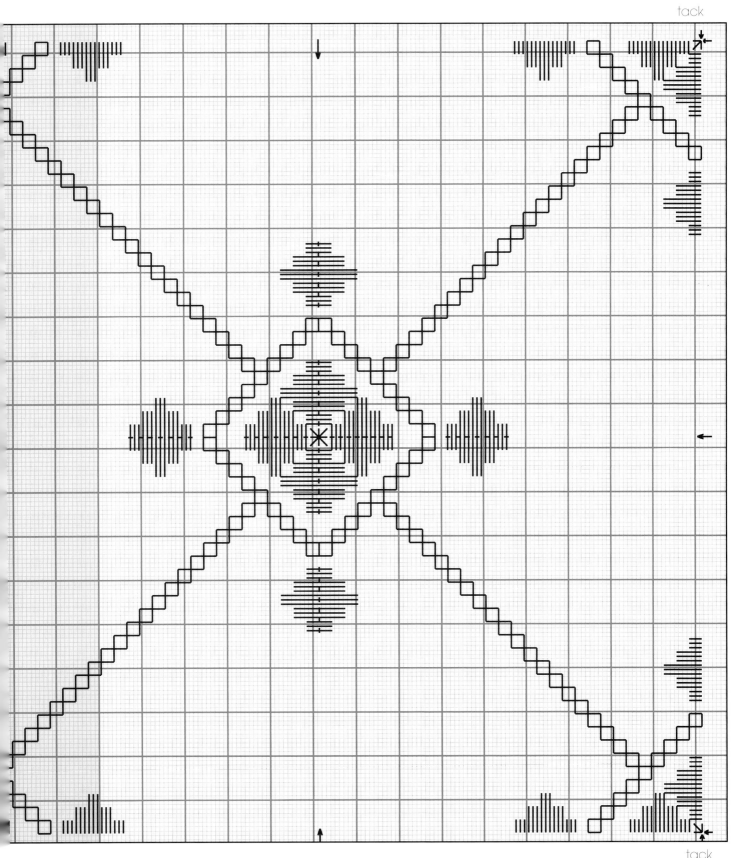

> **Handy Hint** If you want to use four different colours, choose colours that are very light and softly shaded to create a subtle tonal variation. This would also look attractive all stitched in one shade.

Satin *Stitch*

(refer to Chart C)

These motifs are worked using two threads of stranded cotton or silk. I used four different shades of thread, using one thread of gray combined with one thread of Blush for the corners, one thread of gray and one thread of Ice for the centre of each side and one thread each of gray and Crystal Bay for the rest of the satin stitch motifs. To stitch the satin stitch design start at the centre, stitch along one side then turn your work around and stitch back along the other side. Note the dotted line through the centre of the design indicates where each stitch finishes.

Work the satin stitch motifs in the centre of each square and then work the motif found outside the squares - these are all worked in the same shade.

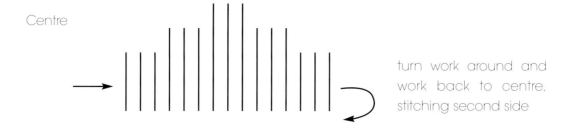

Centre

turn work around and work back to centre, stitching second side

Square Eyelets

Using one thread of the thread used for the satin stitch (if you have changed tones remember to do this for the eyelets also) work the eyelets found in the centre of each satin stitch motif see charts B & C. Refer to page 13 for more information on stitching square eyelets.

Scandanavian Edging Stitch

Count out six threads from the edge of the four sided stitch and work the first row of Scandanavian edging stitch, the stem stitch *on the wrong side* of the fabric. This is worked using two threads of Blush by Waterlilies. Each stitch is worked going forward over six threads and back over three.

The second part of Scandanavian edging has been worked using the thread used for the four sided stitch. Refer to page 18 for more information on stitching Scandanavian edging. Work this round the entire outside edge to complete.

PAUA LIGHTS

Finished! The delicate beauty of Paua Lights will be enjoyed for many years and will become an heirloom for your family and a source of pride for yourself.

CHART C
each line represents one thread

• • • dotted line indicates end of each stitch

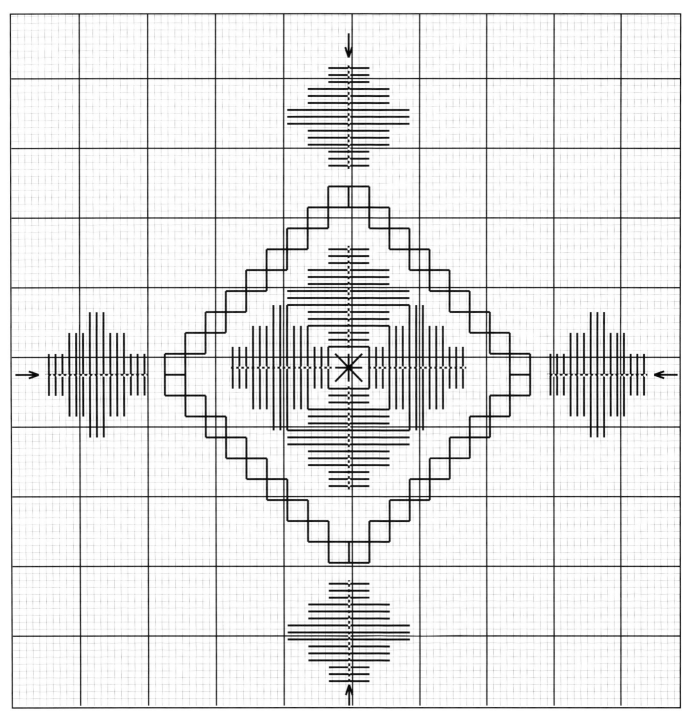

85

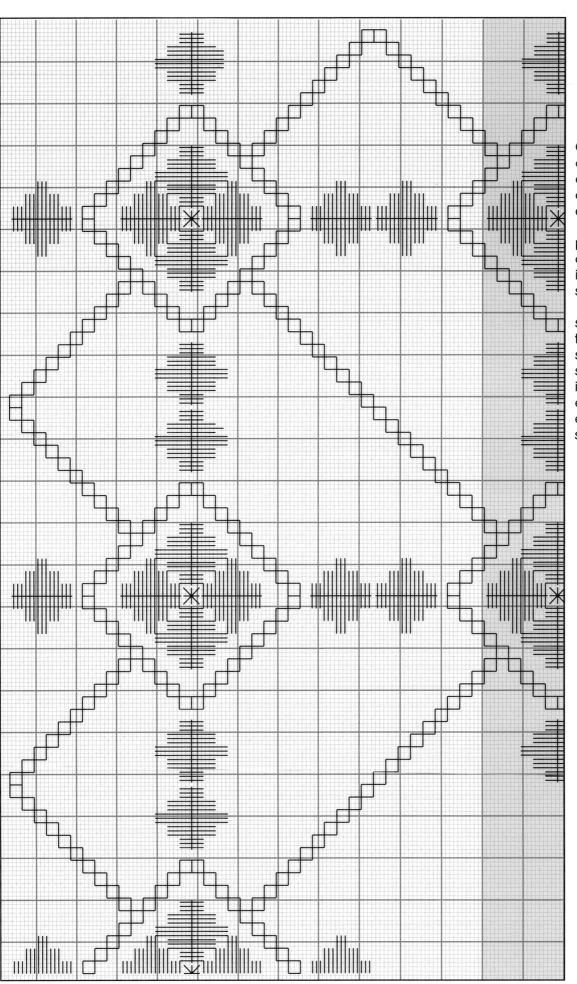

CHART B
one quarter of design

pattern overlap is shaded

solid line through satin stitch indicates end of each stitch

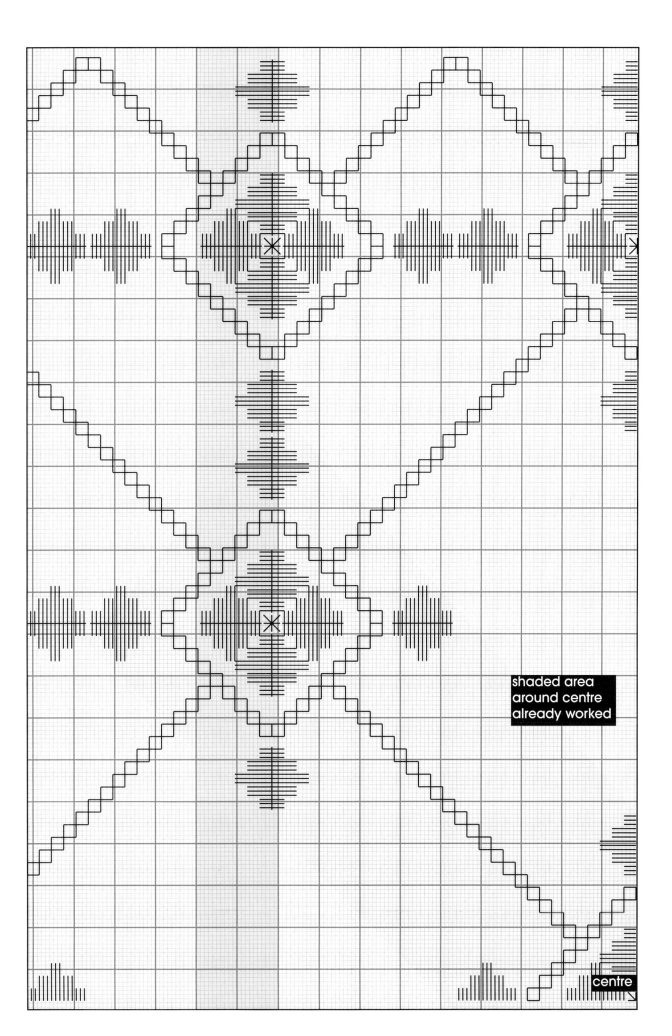

FROM MY HANDS

Blue Horizons
finished size 12 x 47 cms (5 x 18 in)

Auckland is a city situated on an isthmus between two harbours. The sea is all around us and its changing mood is reflected in the changing shades of blue we see.

The sea was the inspiration for the colours used in Blue Horizons but so was a Spanish Sampler stitched in 1729. I have used this Sampler in many different ways. I used the layout as the basis for a very large Sampler I worked using a variety of different counted techniques and since then I have used different parts of the Sampler in many different pieces of embroidery. I rather liked the strong diamond outline in this design but changed the inner design from the original. I worked it on a blue background using 'random' or 'over dyed' blue threads and the subtle tonal changes found in these threads are a feature of this embroidery. It could of course be stitched in many different colour ways on many different coloured linens. The lush fringe and tassels are a rather different treatment to embroidery of this nature and add to its interest.

Stitches used: stem, counted satin, hem, four sided, Holbein and Scandanavian edging stitch

In this pattern four sided and Scandanavian edging stitch are worked over four threads

It is recommended that you stitch this in the sequence given

Materials

- Blue Horizons was stitched on blue Belfast linen with 32 threads to the inch. Other linens could be used, the quantities required are given below:
- linen 30 – 36 threads to the inch - 20 x 65 cm (8 x 26 in)
- linen 25 - 28 threads to the inch - 25 x 70 cm (10 x 28 in)
- Random or 'over dyed' threads were used along with toning stranded threads. We used Fir and Caribbean Waterlilies by Caron. Alternative random dyed threads in suitable shades could be used most satisfactorily. We recommend the use of random dyed threads.
- DMC Perle 8, 932 (light Denim Blue)
- Stranded Cotton or Silk see table use two threads for satin stitch on linen 28 – 36 threads to the inch, three threads for linen 19 –

BLUE HORIZONS

25 threads to the inch.
- Coloured thread for tacking
- tapestry needles No.s 24 or 26
- sharp needle, this can be most useful for finishing off neatly
- 15 cm embroidery hoop

Threads

Fir and Caribbean Waterlilies by Caron

	DMC	Au Ver a Soie D'Alger	Madeira
Sea green	503	1814	1702
Denim Blue	931	1714	1711
Light Denim Blue	932	1713	1710
Sea foam	3752	1712	1002

Instructions

Neaten the raw edges of your fabric, fold it in half lengthwise then tack over and under three threads to mark where the centre of the design will be.

There are four diamonds in Blue Horizons (only two are shown on Chart A). To make your embroidery longer or shorter, stitch more or less diamonds. Chart B gives one pattern repeat in enlarged detail.

Diamond *Outline*

Chart B

Measure 5 cm down the centre line of tacking and following Chart B work the diamond outline. It is stitched in satin stitch using two threads, one thread of Fir and one thread of Sea Green.

Each stitch is worked over six threads. There are three stitches in line at the centre top and bottom but from that point on each stitch is worked by moving two threads down and two threads along. Note at the sides there are three stitches worked over four threads.

Work the diamond outline down the full length of the wall hanging.

Thread two needles and work both sides of the diamond outline at once, this makes it very easy to check that your stitches are in line as you move down the diamond!

When you have completed the satin stitch outline for the diamond design it is edged in stem stitch using one thread of Fir only, going forward four threads and back two. Note it is worked around each diamond shape so that the stem stitching goes between each diamond. For more information on working stem stitch round an outline see page 12.

NB On the side of each diamond the stem stitch is worked two threads beyond the satin stitch so that this outer line of stitching will match the outer point of the cross.

Repeat to extend design

CHART A

Central Cross

Chart B

You may find it helpful to tack in a vertical and horizontal line to indicate the centre of each Diamond. Follow the chart and work the horizontal cross bar in satin stitch using one thread each of Fir and Denim Blue. Start stitching at the centre, work from right to left to complete one side then turn your work 180° and work from the centre out to the other side. Now work the rest of the central cross - working up and down from the horizontal cross bar.

Handy Hint - Turn your work to ensure you are always working satin stitch from right to left.

Starting at the centre, outline the entire cross in stem stitch using one thread of Denim Blue, going forward four threads and coming back two threads. Follow the chart closely when working round the points of the cross.

Work the central crosses first, then work the half and three quarter crosses found at the top, bottom and sides of the hanging.

Wings
Chart B

These are worked in satin stitch using one thread each of Caribbean and light Denim Blue and starting at the right angles of the cross.

Note when working the wings that you move one thread over in the centre but two out on the outer edge until you are covering 12 threads. At this point watch the pattern carefully as you only move out one more thread on the outside for the next two rows. The detail worked at the edge of each wing is worked in Holbein stitch using the same two threads - with each stitch worked over two threads.

Sides

There are four rows of stem stitch worked down each side of the design. Work these from the inside edge to the outside edge, starting two threads from the edge of the diamond. Each row is worked two threads apart.

Row 1	one thread of Caribbean
Row 2	one thread of Sea Foam
Row 3	one thread of light Denim Blue
Row 4	one thread each of Fir and Sea Green

To finish *the sides*

Work the first row of Scandanavian edging stitch, the stem stitch, *on the wrong side* of the design, six threads out from the last row of stem stitch using two threads of light Denim Blue stranded cotton or one thread of light Denim Blue DMC Perle 8. Each stitch is worked going forward over eight threads and back over four. Start at the top edge and finish just below the satin stitching at the base of the design.

The second row of Scandanavian edging stitch has been worked using two threads of light Denim Blue stranded. Refer to page 18 for more information on stitching Scandanavian edging stitch. To ensure that the edging stitches on both sides line up, run a tacking thread across the top from the first side to the starting position of the second side.

CHART B one pattern – repeat
each line represents one thread

Pattern overlap shaded

— indicates end of each stitch

BLUE HORIZONS

To finish the base

Work four sided stitch over four threads across the base of the hanging *between* the Scandanavian edging stitch on each side. It is worked using two threads of light Denim Blue stranded cotton or one thread of DMC Perle 8. Pull out all the threads beyond the stitching to make the fringe. To make a truly luxuriant fringe extra threads are added.

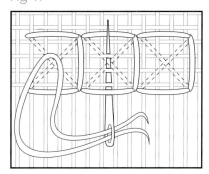

Fig 1.

To do this, cut lengths of thread using all the colours used in the embroidery, a little longer than the desired length of the fringe. Thread the *two ends* of a length of thread through the eye of the needle. Take your needle up under the bottom stitch in your four sided stitch edging and pick up a small amount of fabric, (fig 1.) then take your needle back through the thread loop and pull down firmly (fig 2). Position the knot at the base of the hanging. Do this between each stitch and into each stitch all the way across the bottom of the hanging.

Tassels

Use approximately twelve threads of varying weights (all the strands of Waterlilies or stranded cotton count as one thread for the tassel!) and cut the thread for four tassels with a finished length of 15 cm and two tassels with a finished length of 18 cm. The shorter tassels are placed at the top and centre and the longer tassels are placed nearer the lower edge (see colour photograph page 54 for placement). Plait the first third of each tassel before positioning where indicated. Attach by taking the threads used to tie the tassel together through to the back of your hanging and fasten off either with a knot or finish the threads in the usual manner.

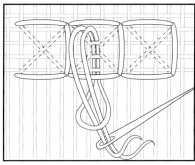

Fig 2.

Top

Fold in the raw edge then fold over the top fabric leaving enough space to thread the hanger through. Hem stitch in place using matching thread (one thread of stranded cotton or silk). A wooden or bamboo skewer makes a good hanger! Plait a length of fine cord using the threads from your embroidery and knot each end. Attach to the back of your embroidery, wrap the cord around the tassels at each side of the top and bring the cord up in the centre.

Now hang your finished embroidery in a prominent position, feel proud of your accomplishment, and enjoy it! You are continuing a tradition begun by another needle woman almost 300 years ago.

Danish Handkerchief
finished size 36 cm (14 in) square

The starting point for this 'handkerchief' was a postcard that I bought while travelling in Denmark. The postcard showed a seventeenth century 'handkerchief' with this pattern around the edge. Handkerchiefs in this period had a broader range of uses than we now give them. They were more our scarf size and were used for covering and wrapping food, as small table cloths etc.

Not long after returning home I worked with magnifying glass and graph paper and charted one corner and the border from the postcard. I was really thrilled to be able to create this beautiful design and stitched it using the very best linen and silk thread that I could buy.

It is shown with a cup of tea and chocolates, it would also be superb as a table centre for a special dinner where all the embroidery would be seen and admired! Stitch coasters and serviettes to match repeating the star on the coasters (see pattern page 36) and the corner design on the serviettes to create an heirloom for your home.

Stitches used: counted or geometric satin stitch, four sided stitch, Scandanavian edging stitch, Holbein, circular eyelets and stem stitch

In this pattern the Scandanavian edging stitch and four sided stitch are worked over three threads

It is recommended that you stitch the design in the sequence given

Materials

- 'Fine thread*' this is used as a general term to apply to thread, the weight and appearance of sewing cotton but either 100% cotton, silk or linen which is chosen to match the fabric, see table. It is used for eyelet, four sided stitch and the second part of Scandanavian edging stitch. If a heavier thread is preferred DMC Coton a broder 25 may be used for the four sided and Scandanavian edging stitches (see 'Instructions'). Alternative fabrics and the threads to use with them are given in the table
- Matching stranded cotton or silk is used for the satin, stem and Holbein stitching
- Matching Perle 12 for the first part of Scandanavian edging stitch
- Tapestry Needles Size 24 or 26, sharp needle for starting & finishing
- Contrast tacking thread
- 15 cm embroidery hoop

FROM MY HANDS

Instructions

The chart for this design is large - we give one quarter of the design in Chart A. To work the design refer to the smaller charts which accompany each part of the project.

Neaten the raw edges of your linen.
The Scandanavian edging stitch is worked last.
Work all the four sided stitch on this design before working the satin stitch, eyelets or stem stitch.
Start working the four sided stitch in one corner and work all that corner. Then work the side band and the next corner, continue in this

A Danish Handkerchief

linen cream	'fine thread*'	matching stranded cotton or silk	
quantity required - numbers in bold equal threads per inch	threads for four sided stitch, eyelets, 2nd part of Scandinavian edging stitch.	threads for counted satin stitch	threads for 1st part of Scandinavian edging stitch
35 cream 28 - 35 **50** cm sq (20 in sq)	• Zwicky 100% cotton or silk • *Guterman 100 % silk or cotton* • Au Ver a Soie 1003 100% silk • Madeira Cotona • Kreinik one ply of Serica • Dewhurst Sylko • Londonderry linen thread 100/3 • DMC Dentelles 80 for fabric with 19 - 30 threads per inch	two threads used **D** Ecru **Av** F 1 **M** Ecru **A** 926 **Kr** Cream	**D** *Perle 12* **Av** Perlee **Kr** Serica **L** 80/3
25 55 cm sq (22 in sq) **19** 80 cm sq 30 in sq	• DMC Perle 12 • Coton a broder 25 • Londonderry linen thread 50/3	use three threads for satin stitch on fabric with 19 - 25 threads per inch.	**D** Perle 5 or 8 **L** 30/3 **Kr** Serica

D = DMC **Av** = Au Ver a Soie D'Alger **Kr** = Kreinik Mori **M** = Madeira **L** = Londonderry **A** = Anchor

• The availability of threads varies around the world. We give alternatives which we know will give equal satisfaction in their use and create an equally beautiful design for you.
• Materials used shown in italics.

DANISH HANDKERCHIEFS

way until all the four sided stitch is completed. Work from right to left and hold your embroidery so that you are working towards yourself.

All four sided stitching is sewn in the same way. I like to sew it with fine silk, cotton, or linen thread and to achieve the crisp, precise finish which I like, I work each stitch twice. Do not sew one four sided stitch and then go back and sew again on top of the first stitch as this will not give the correct tension, rather embroider each part of the stitch twice as you are working it. If you would rather not do this use DMC Coton a broder 25 and then double stitching will not be required. Sew over three threads at all times.

CHART A
This shows one quarter of the design

FROM MY HANDS

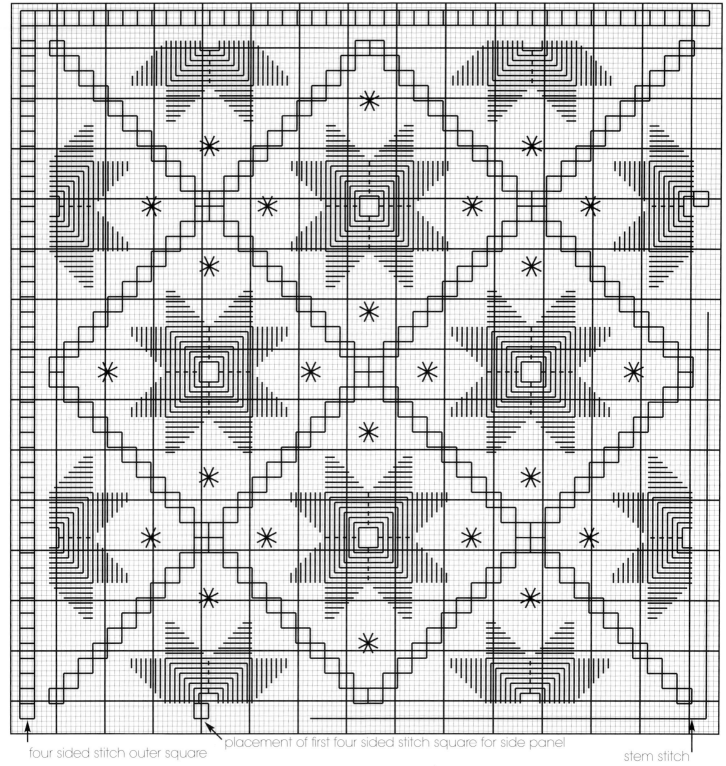

four sided stitch outer square · placement of first four sided stitch square for side panel · stem stitch

Four Sided Stitch Outer Square

(Chart B)

Four sided stitch is worked right round the entire design, creating an outer square. Start in one corner using the long thread method (see page 11). Measure in 2 cm from each edge and work four sided stitch, over three threads, out from the corner in both directions for more than half the width of the mat.

CHART B
corner pattern

start in corner

each line represents one thread

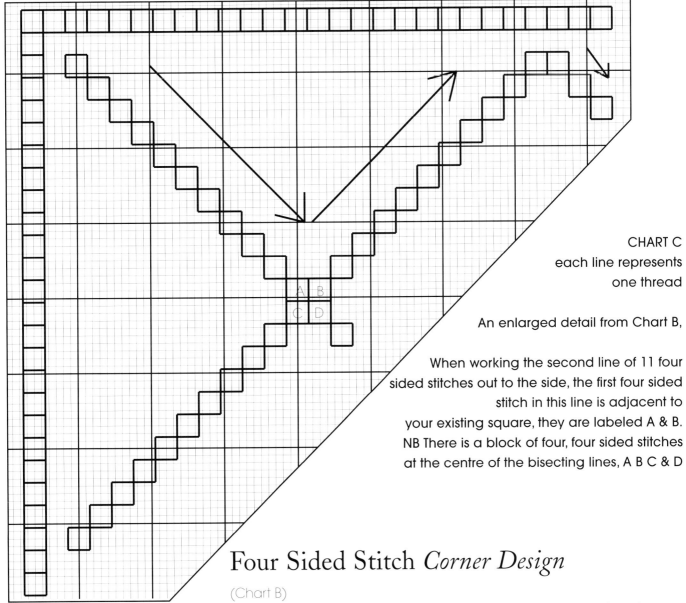

CHART C
each line represents
one thread

An enlarged detail from Chart B,

When working the second line of 11 four sided stitches out to the side, the first four sided stitch in this line is adjacent to your existing square, they are labeled A & B.
NB There is a block of four, four sided stitches at the centre of the bisecting lines, A B C & D

Four Sided Stitch *Corner Design*

(Chart B)

To stitch the pulled thread corner design, count in three threads from the four sided stitch outline on both sides. A small section of Chart B is shown *in enlarged detail* in Chart C to help you get started, refer to this to work the first 11 four sided stitches out from the corner, on the diagonal. (see page 18 for detailed information on working four sided stitch on the diagonal).

Next work 11 more four sided stitches out to the side, note the position the first four sided stitch in this line is worked in - it is adjacent to your existing square (squares A & B). On completion of the row you should be three threads away from the four sided stitch outline - a handy check that all the stitches have been worked correctly. Now continue to work along the side following the chart, checking that you finish each time three threads from the initial row of four sided stitch. The order of working the four sided stitch out from the corner is shown in fig. 1.

Return to the corner and work out in the other direction in the same way. Note there is a block of four, four sided stitches at the centre of the bisecting lines, (squares A, B, C & D).

Complete the balance of the four sided stitch in each corner. Work out from the corner diagonal line and then branch to each side.

Four sided stitch Side Panels

(one half of the side panel is shown on Chart D)
Now work the four sided stitch in the side panels up to the next corner. You will find it helpful to run a tacking thread over and under three threads from the centre of the half diamond at the side out to the starting position for the four sided stitch worked along the side of the design (refer back to Chart B). The first diagonal line of four sided stitch comes towards the centre.
Note carefully where to start the first four sided stitch.

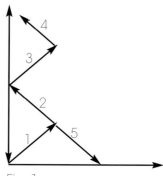

Fig. 1
This shows the order to work four sided stitch out from the corner

When you have completed this, stitch the next corner in the same way that you stitched the first. Continue in this way until you have completed all the four sided stitch for the entire design.

Stem Stitch and Holbein stitch corner design

Chart D shows the stem stitch on one quarter of the design. An enlarged detail of the Holbein stitch motif is shown on Chart E.
Stem stitch is worked around the inner edge of the design and the inner and outer edges of the side panel. It is stitched using two threads of matching stranded cotton or silk. Stitch the Holbein stitch motif when you reach it. The stem stitch is worked three threads beyond the four sided stitch and each stitch is worked by going forward six threads and coming back three threads. Start stitching close to a corner, with the stem stitches positioned directly beneath the four sided stitches, (fig. 2). (See Chart D for starting position.)

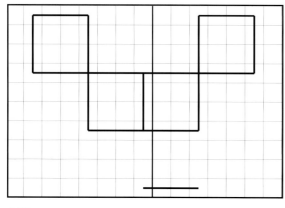

Fig. 2
shows how to position the stem stitch beneath four sided stitch

DANISH HANDKERCHIEFS

Satin Stitch Stars
Chart F

Work the four complete satin stitch stars found in the centre of each diamond. To ensure correct placement of the stars you may find it

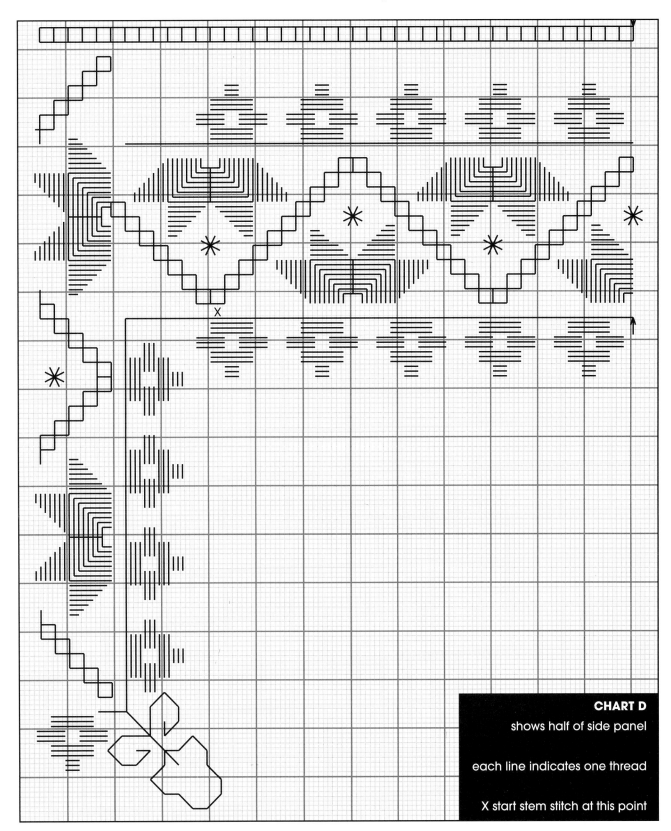

CHART D

shows half of side panel

each line indicates one thread

X start stem stitch at this point

helpful to quickly run a tacking thread over and under three threads from point to point, refer to fig. 3.

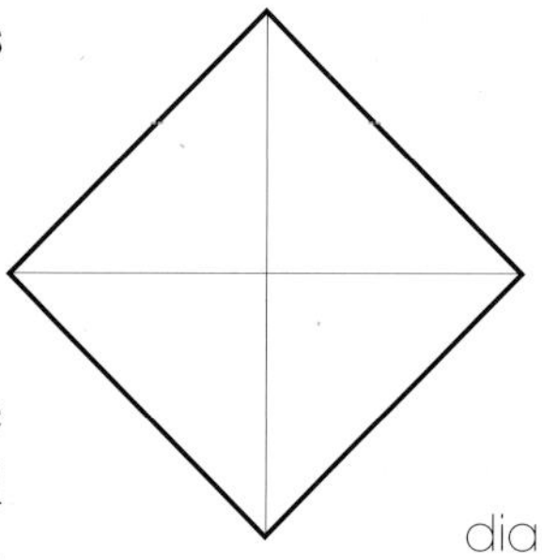

To stitch the satin stitch stars use two threads of stranded cotton or silk that matches your fabric and refer to Chart F where the star is shown in detail. Start at the centre of the star working one segment of the star at a time. The first stitch is over two threads and in the following rows, one side of the star is kept straight, whilst on the other side one more thread is picked up each line. At the eighth row this is reversed and the side that was straight now decreases one thread per line and the other side has a straight edge. When you have completed one segment of the star take your needle under the stitching at the back of your work to the centre ready to being the next segment. Complete the star.

Fig. 3
A diamond with tacking thread from point to point for correct placement of star

Half *Stars*

(refer to charts B and D for their placement)

You may find it easier to position these correctly if you run a tacking thread from the central point of the four sided stitch diamond, to the four sided stitch squares at the outer edge and the stem stitch on the inner side. Count in three threads from the line of four sided stitch or stem stitch, and work the sections of the half star following the chart.

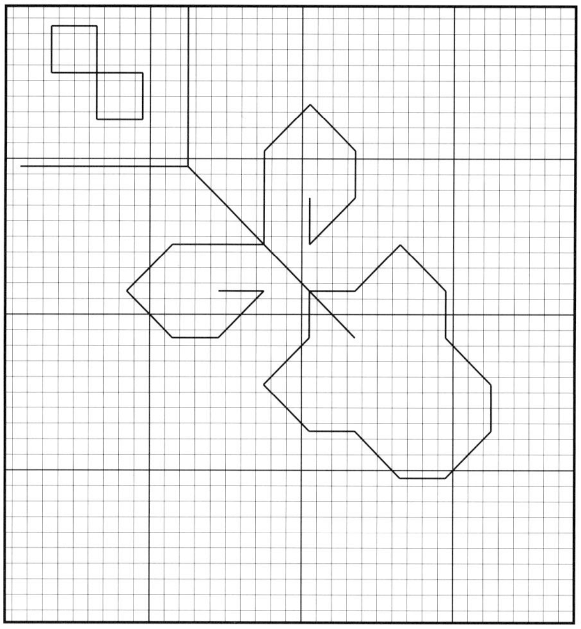

Satin Stitch Block Pattern

(refer to chart D for placement)

Using two threads of stranded silk or cotton, follow chart D and work this pattern along both sides of the stem stitch border. Although it looks as though it is worked directly on top of the stem stitch there is actually one thread between the stem stitch and the blocks of satin stitch

Eyelets

(refer to chart F)

The eyelets are worked using the fine thread used for the four sided stitch or one thread of stranded cotton or silk. They are not stitched twice. All the eyelets in this embroidery are stitched with the centre of the eyelet lined up with the centre of the diamond four sided stitch outline and with the top of the fourth four sided stitch counting from the point. See the arrows on Chart F. Refer to page 14 for detailed information on stitching circular eyelets.

Chart E
The Holbein stitch motif

DANISH HANDKERCHIEFS

Scandanavian *Edging Stitch*

The first line of this stitch is worked *six threads beyond* the line of four sided stitch *on the wrong side* of the embroidery. To create a little more texture along the edge it is stitched using matching Perle 12 thread going forward six threads and coming back three. Line the stitching up directly beneath the four sided stitch and start near a corner.

The second journey of this stitch is worked using the fine thread used in your four sided stitch. For detailed information on working Scandanavian edging stitch refer to page 18.

This exquisite design, created by your hands, is a masterpiece in design and technique. It is a pleasure to present it to you for your stitching enjoyment.

CHART F each line represents one thread

••• dotted line indicates end of each stitch

Enlarged detail showing the star and placement of eyelets

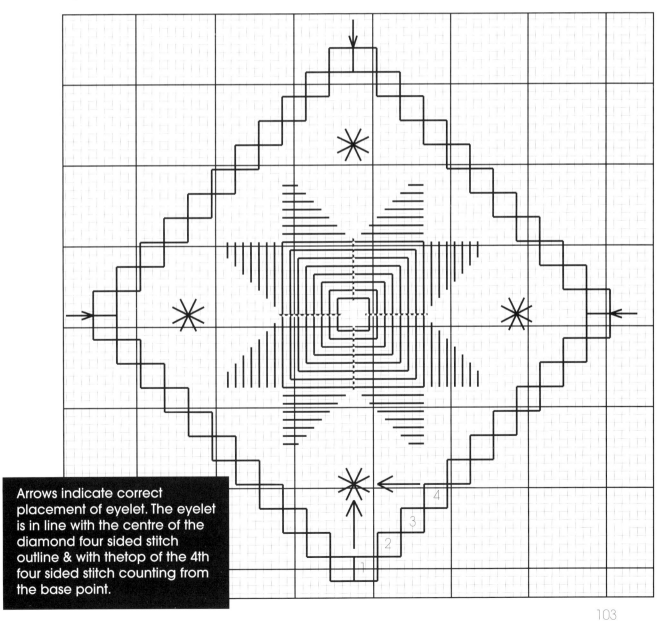

Arrows indicate correct placement of eyelet. The eyelet is in line with the centre of the diamond four sided stitch outline & with thetop of the 4th four sided stitch counting from the base point.